PARISHES AND CHURCHES
IN
ROMNEY MARSH

PARISHES AND CHURCHES IN ROMNEY MARSH

Harvey Van Sickle

Drawings by
Peter Kent

Ronald Spinney and
The Romney Marsh Historic Churches Trust

© Ronald Spinney, 1991

First published 1991.
by Ronald Spinney, The Orchard, Blackheath, London
and The Romney Marsh Historic Churches Trust.

All rights reserved.
Unauthorised duplication contravenes applicable laws.

ISBN 0 9517559 0 0

Printed and bound in Great Britain by
Felton Litho, 47 Eastcastle Street, London W1N 7PF

CONTENTS

FOREWORD 5

PARISHES AND CHURCHES

Introduction 7
Ecclesiastical Parishes 11
Civil Parishes 17
The Marsh and its Owners 21
Churches and Change 27

THE CHURCHES

St Peter and St Paul, Bilsington 34
St Rumwold, Bonnington 36
St Eanswith, Brenzett 38
St Augustine, Brookland 41
All Saints, Burmarsh 44
St Peter and St Paul, Dymchurch 46
St Mary, East Guldeford 48
St Thomas-a-Becket, Fairfield 50
St George, Ivychurch 52
All Saints, Lydd 55
St Peter and St Paul, Newchurch 58
St Nicholas, New Romney 60
St Clement, Old Romney 62
St Mary Magdalene, Ruckinge 64
St Mary, Rye 66
St Mary the Virgin, St Mary in the Marsh 69
St Dunstan, Snargate 72
St Augustine, Snave 74

CHRONOLOGY 77

GLOSSARY 83

BIBLIOGRAPHY AND FURTHER READING 89

INDEX 93

All Saints, Lydd

FOREWORD

Since my family and I discovered Romney Marsh nearly twenty years ago, I have been fascinated by the Marsh Churches - by their architecture, the diversity of their sizes, and their apparent loneliness. I was particularly intrigued to know why there were so many churches for such a small population, and so I asked Harvey Van Sickle if he would research and write this book, and Peter Kent if he would draw the churches.

I hope you get as much pleasure out of the result as I have.

There are a number of people I must thank, especially Mrs Jill Eddison of the Romney Marsh Research Trust, Dr N. P. Hudd and Mr Ralph Carter of the Romney Marsh Historic Churches Trust for their comments and suggestions on the text, and Peter Godfrey for his help in the printing. However, my principal thanks must go to Harvey Van Sickle for such a lucid and informative text, and Peter Kent for his sketches which catch the mood of the churches so well.

Ronald Spinney
April, 1991

INTRODUCTION

The existence of parishes in England tends to be taken for granted: they simply exist, all over the country; they were clearly the focus of social life in early times; and in some areas they formed (and still form) the basis of local government. Like most institutions, however, parishes are much more complex than they seem at first glance.

Understandably, histories of particular parishes tend to deal mainly with the religious parish and the church, starting with the first record of its existence (often 1086, the date of Domesday) and moving on to the development of the existing building. Reference is often made to the local civil community - the Lord of the Manor, major landowners, and important noble families - but the church's relation to local government, as it were, is most often passed over in favour of a more church-centred study.

The interaction between the religious and civil life of the parish, however, probably had the greatest impact upon the building and embellishment of local churches as we know them. Especially in areas as remote and independent as the Romney Marsh, the parish church was more than just the centre of religious life: it was the focus of a complex, coherent, and very sophisticated system of organising all aspects of mediaeval life - social, religious, political and moral. The remains of our churches are now, arguably, the only major physical evidence left of this system.

An important point to understand is that the forerunners of the civil parishes generally predate the religious parishes of the country. This may at first seem odd, but it is because the ecclesiastical parishes had to fit within an existing system of feudal land control; the first parishes were thus often, or even usually, co-terminus with the boundaries of an existing manorial holding.

This was simply a factor of feudal life: without an income, a site for a church, and the labour to erect a building, the parish church could not exist. Initially at least, it was dependent upon the local feudal Lord (or thane) for these prerequisites, and in exchange the landowner usually reserved the right to nominate the local priest. In some cases - and in Romney Marsh fairly frequently - the church was established directly by the bishop or a monastery, as he or it had become the landlord when the estate was given to them by the king or a noble. In these cases, the bishop or institution was simply lord of the manor: the relationship between owner and parish remained the same.

Another important point is that the thane or Lord - or whoever controlled the local community and the appointment of the parish priest - was part of an inherently religious society. The pious contribution of the lord may have had either high or low motives, but it was not undertaken either lightly or merely as some sort of burden which came along with other earthly duties. Early wills leaving bequests for prayers, chantry chapels, alms and the like are striking: it is clear that these are the religious offerings of people who are in true mortal fear for the fate of their souls. This is somewhat difficult to comprehend in our science-based age, perhaps, and such bequests are often cynically dismissed as the leaving behind of impressive monuments to earthly accomplishments. They did, of course, often have this effect, but more often were too small or private to be anything other than truly spiritual in nature.

To understand some of the nuances of this relationship in pre-Reformation parishes, it is essential to understand the nature of ecclesiastical and civil parishes (including the latter's predecessors, the manors). Unfortunately, the general relationship between the two has not been well explored by historians, and even the local government role of parish vestries was largely unstudied until the 19th century.

This singular lack of interest seems to have been rooted in the fact that the parish vestry had no statutory basis: it was a remnant of the feudal system of manorial law, overlaid by the later system of ecclesiastical parishes as the natural unit of local control. If understandable in terms of legal history, however, the neglect of the fundamental importance of the parish is still remarkable. As Bryan Keith-Lucas has written in his work on early local government:

"At a time when the greater part of the population had no means of transport other than their own two legs and when, under the laws of 'settlement', the ordinary people of England were bound by invisible but powerful bonds to the parish to which they belonged, the parish vestry and its officers inevitably mattered in many ways far more than Parliament or the king."

Clearly, some understanding of the development of civil and ecclesiastical parishes is important for anyone interested in the phenomenon of local churches. Our churches were not erected in isolation: they were not built as academic exercises in architectural design, nor as repositories for genealogical archives. They were, rather, the focus of both the religious and civil aspects of life, and for most of their history these two aspects were simply indivisible. Even the local rector tended to be nominated by the major local landowner; indeed, and particularly in smaller holdings which fell to the younger sons of landed families, the rector and the local landowner were often one and the same person.

Since the religious parish had to fit from the start within the existing manorial/township system, no real division existed in the early stages between the two as far as the life of the local community was concerned. Granted, the civil township and the religious parishes tended to grow apart over time, as manors were subdivided, parish boundaries were altered, and larger towns developed. This later development is of less significance than it seems for churches, however, as most of the inherent attraction of parish churches to the casual visitor tends to have been created during the earlier, more cohesive period of the parish's existence. This cohesion lasted for hundreds of years, and one could maintain that at least until the Reformation of the early 1500s the two sides of the parish coin were indivisible.

Certainly the eventual development of the parish vestry as the main element of local government shows such a system, as various parish officers took on roles which shifted between the religious and the civil. The gradual process by which separate civil and ecclesiastical institutions developed can be glimpsed in many areas: to give three examples, one can look at language history and the nature of two ancient parochial offices. In the first case (that of language), it is significant that Old English had no term for the physical area known to the Normans as a "parish", even though the system of ecclesiastical parishes had developed by about 1000 A.D. The old term, priest-shire or shrift-shire, really dealt with the legal sense of a priest's jurisdictional area, as distinct from that of the local lord, and the term "parish" is, in fact, not recorded until the 1200s.

The shifting and fluent nature of the dividing line between civil and religious parishes is also seen in the gradual shift of local administration to the parish constable from his manorial equivalent, but within the area of the parish rather than the manor. The manorial bailiff had been appointed by the Lord of the Manor; the constable, a local policeman/administrator, was appointed by the parish vestry or – as it could be an unpopular task – was taken in turn by the local population. The basic role, however, remained the same.

A similar change can be seen with church wardens: these retained their responsibility for guarding and maintaining the church, but the role was eventually changed to a purely lay office, with the wardens being appointed by the open local meeting known as the parish vestry. Even the "vestry" is significant in this context: this body of local government, dealing solely with matters temporal, developed its name by the early 1500s by virtue of the general practice of holding its meetings in that room of the church.

The following two chapters examine the development of ecclesiastical and civil parishes; the division into two parts, however, should not obscure the central point that for most inhabitants, the two were much the same creature.

St Nicholas, New Romney

ECCLESIASTICAL PARISHES

The religious parish in England has existed as part of the cultural landscape for some 1,200 years - so long a period that its existence has come to seem almost as natural a feature as the very stones of the earth themselves. This familiar aspect of local parishes tends to hide the fact that they were, in fact, the result of the radical introduction of Christianity into a settled pagan landscape.

Parishes were a development of the earliest administrative structures of the Christian church, and represent the second stage of Christianity. In the earliest days - the missionary phase, lasting from Augustine's arrival in 597 to the middle of the 600s - the church basically operated as a single, unitary diocese. As bishop, Augustine was assisted by his priests in the countryside, housed in minsters; other priests acted as assistants, as required, but the entire community of priests lived at the minsters and travelled out to convert the population.

This pattern worked very well for conversion, but was unsuitable for day-to-day pastoral care. Some sort of subdivision of the diocese was clearly needed, and the eventual system - with a priest in every village to preach, celebrate and baptise - was recognised as the only real solution by as early a writer as Bede (who noted this in a letter to Egbert, the Archbishop of York, in 734).

The church's administrative structure was reorganised by Theodore, the Archbishop of Canterbury from 668 to 690, but it was to be another century or more before parishes were established in earnest. Nonetheless, the selection of Kent for Augustine's mission meant that the county holds most of the earliest English churches: as John Newman points out in "The Buildings of England", the remains of only 10 churches of the 600s exist in the country and just one - Bradwell, in Essex - is found outside of Kent.

Regardless, then, precisely when the religious parish was established - after, or along with the first settlement of the land - it is clear that early Saxon churches had to fit within a recently-converted or even pagan landscape. There had, however, long been a system of "proprietary churches" in pagan Teutonic society, whereby the land-lord (or thane) was bound to provide a priest and a temple for his dependants' worship. The conversion of the country was obviously simplified if this accepted social duty of the lord was simply transferred from the pagan to the Christian church.

The basic problem facing the church was thus one of access to land, income and the population, and the solution - to have the churches founded by each seigneurial lord - was developed in the early 800s by Charlemagne and his successor, Louis I. During the next century, village churches began to appear throughout northern Europe, and although further developments were delayed by the collapse in the late 800s of the first Holy Roman Empire, the system was re-established along with the new, feudal-based Holy Roman Empire founded in 962.

The building and endowment of churches and rectorships in England followed Charlemagne's principles quite closely, with the priest being given the control and income from the glebe lands, the tithe, and offerings for special services (the saying of prayers, blessings, etc.). The principles were reinforced by canon laws passed by Ethelred the Unready (979-1014) and his successful challenger, Cnut (1016-1035), and were primarily as follows:

- Every church had its lord – either a thane, a group of freemen, or the king.

- The lord had to build a church (or supply the means to do so), but then could neither pull it down nor use it for other purposes.

- Upkeep of the church was the responsibility of the bishop, but came out of the tithes, thus ensuring that the parish shared in the upkeep of the building.

- The lord retained the right to choose the priest, and the method of selection. (Originally, many rectorships were made hereditary).

- The bishop retained the right to disapprove of the lord's nominee, but only on the grounds of unsoundness in faith or morals.

- The clergy remained under the authority of the bishop with regards to attendance at synod, ordination for office, etc.

- Once nominated by the lord and appointed by the bishop, the clergy could not be removed by the lord (known as "freehold of the clergy").

- The priest had to service all of the inhabitants of the feudal estate – he had the care, or "cure" of their souls – and could undertake private services only if licensed to do so by the bishop.

- The lord had the right to receive an annual rent from the priest – usually money, but occasionally services.

- The lord's rights of nomination and rent could be transferred by sale, gift or bequest, in whole or in part.

In England, the system of establishing – and, perhaps even more importantly, of endowing – manorial parishes first became official with the passing of laws in the mid 900s which made the paying of tithes to the church obligatory. The first statute was passed by Edmund (939-946), and provided for ecclesiastical penalties; his son Edgar (959-975) added temporal penalties.

Edmund and Edgar's laws appear, however, to be a codifying of accepted nobles' practice rather than a new imposition by the crown upon feudal lords: a document of the mid-1000s notes that the existence of a church on a noble's estate could be taken as one of the signs of thanely rank. Thus official encouragement joined forces with pious conversion and feudal display to cover the settled landscape with parish priests and churches.

It must be stressed that this provision of churches and priests was not in any way divorced from civil life, nor was it primarily a form of social duty largely unrelated to piety: the two were indivisible.

In addition, and aside from the fact that bequests in ancient wills show true pious concern with the fate of souls, the establishment of churches must certainly have been closely tied to the accepted principle that the crown was held by divine sanction. The unquestioned idea that one of the major works of god was the provision of princes and kings was not, of course, a Christian idea, as its roots lay in pagan kingship rights. Thus the establishment and embellishment of a parish church by a local lord or noble benefactor had long combined spiritual and civil duties: given that the lord's temporal authority came from the king, and that the king's ultimate authority came from god (whether pagan or Christian), it was clearly the lord's duty to respect his own "delegated divine right" by providing and embellishing his local subjects' place of worship.

The church was, of course, a willing participant in this system, as it was the best way to establish local churches. As shown, populated land was invariably controlled by a lord, and income, a site and the labour to erect a building could not be obtained without the lord's consent. In addition to this practical consideration, however, a major advantage to the church of the manorial based parish system was that it expanded naturally as more land was settled and brought under cultivation. Many new estates were established by Ethelred (979-1016), not least in an attempt to fund and man his wars against the Danes; since each new lord then had to provide a church and tithes, the church had an official and efficient way of moving hand-in-hand with the thanes into newly-settled areas.

A stable method of founding parishes had thus developed, and it is significant that the majority of old parish churches in England were founded in the years between 900 and 1200. Much of this had to do with the continuing formation of new feudal estates, with particular activity during the reigns of Edward the Confessor (1042-1066) and the first two Williams (1066-1100). In addition, and following the lead of the king, many of the thanes' rights of nomination to and income from the local church were granted to monasteries and cathedrals as pious offerings - by far the main source of such rights held by bishops and monasteries.

Given the need to establish his authority after the Conquest, it is hardly surprising to find that William formed a great number of new landholdings, and that this led to an extended period of church building and rebuilding in the Norman style. The parishes of Romney Marsh provide something of a microcosm of this sequence of church building.

Many of the Romney Marsh manors - such as Ruckinge, Snave, Burmarsh and Aldington - are recorded well into Saxon times: Ruckinge to 791, for example, and Burmarsh to 848. Such churches thus appear to have had a very early origin, and may well have been founded at the same time as the manor. Others, however, appear to follow the pattern of "manor-first-church-later".

In the absence of references in various documents, the dating of churches from other than extant building remains is notoriously difficult. The dedication of a church can give some idea, however, particularly when it is to a Saxon saint. Thus Brookland and Snave churches, which are both dedicated to St. Augustine, could well date to the establishment of the local manorial estate - particularly when, as in the case of Snave, the manor was held prior to the mid 800s by Augustine's abbey itself. Snargate, however, is dedicated to St. Dunstan, who died in 988 - over a century after the first known reference to one of the manors included within its parochial boundaries.

A - Orgarswick
B - Blackmanstone

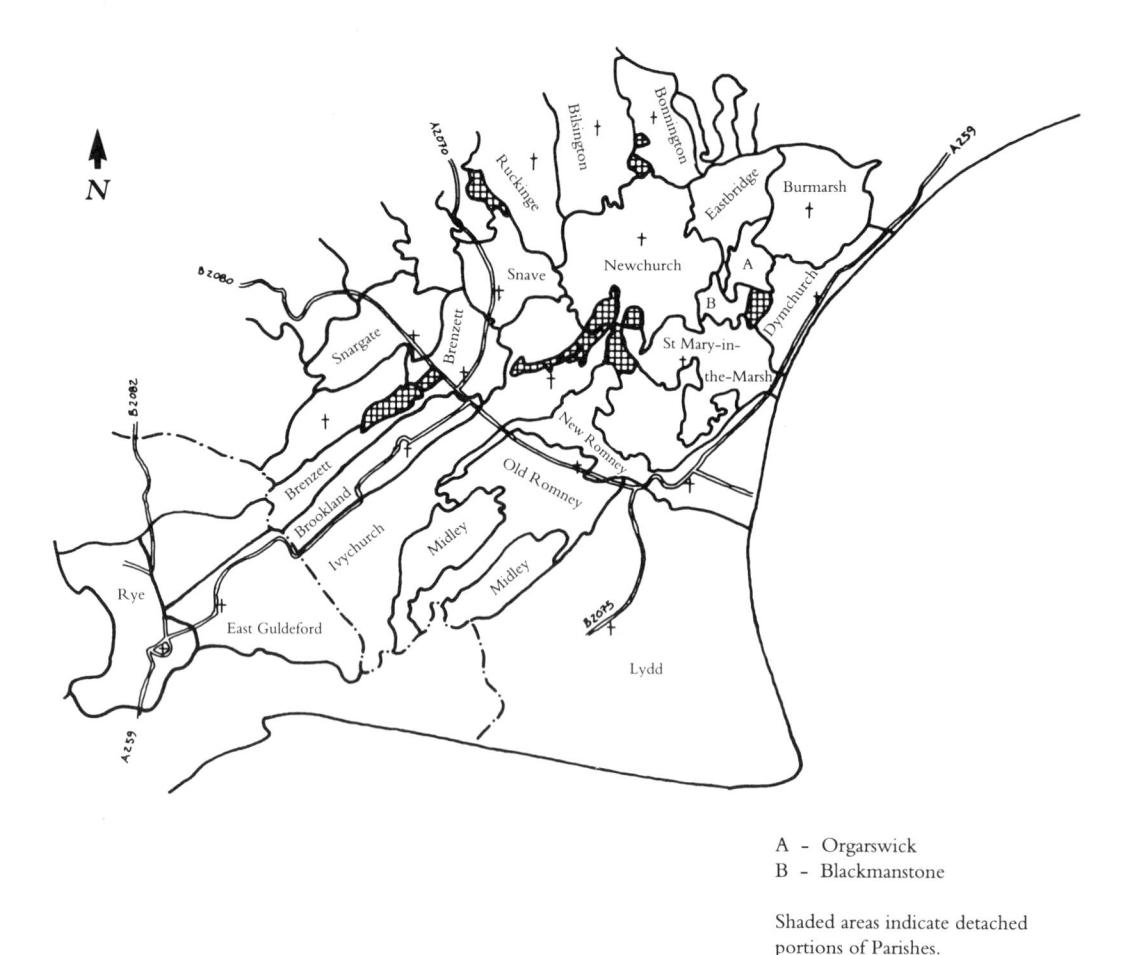

Shaded areas indicate detached portions of Parishes.

Map 1 - Parishes in Romney Marsh

Many of the churches were, of course, established as the manorial population increased and additional churches were required. This is probably the case for a church such as Fairfield, which is dedicated to St. Thomas-a-Beckett: this suggests a foundation date after his martyrdom of 1170, since once dedicated, one seldom finds a church being re-dedicated to another saint. (Ivychurch may, however, be the exception to this rule: the building has foundations of the 1200s, but the dedication to St. George suggests a complete re-establishment after the founding of the Order of the Garter in 1350. It is significant that the existing building dates to c.1360.)

This supplying of churches for each new or established estate also explains the remarkable number of parish churches in the Marsh - an area, like the fens of Lincolnshire, where there is no record of a population to require so much accommodation, and where some parishes never have had more than a few families at any given date. Basically, however, there was one church per manor, regardless of the population of the estate. Thus the critical factor in determining the number of parish churches was not the size of the population: as each estate had a church, and became a parish, it was the nature of the land and the number of estates which it could support. It is no coincidence that one finds most such churches - ones without an obvious local population to demand a large building - precisely in areas with rich alluvial soils which have been reclaimed from rivers and fens.

The main boundaries of the manorial parish network were settled in 1289, with the passing by Edward I of a statute which forbade the creation of new freehold tenants by local lords: without free tenants, a manorial court could not be held, and without a court a manor had virtually no enforceable rights.

This was the end of feudal land settlement, and the start of a long process by which existing manorial rights withered away. As pointed out below, this process lasted formally for over 600 years, with the remnants of manorial holdings not being officially wound up until the Property Acts of the 1920s. In the meantime, however, the old parochial system was remarkably efficient in supplying pastoral care to the countryside. The ancient parishes provided sufficient churches to service the population until the industrial revolution, and it was not until the 19th century that extensive new church and parish creation acts were required.

During this long history, however, the main effects of having a feudal-based church network lay in the embellishment of buildings and the right of presentation to the living of the rectorship. In spite of its antiquity, this practice of a lay person owning the advowson - a transferable and saleable right to nominate the local priest - is surely one of the oddest wrinkles of church administration; not suprisingly, it led to a number of peculiarities.

A true rector is an ordained priest who holds the "benefice" of his office - the freehold of the parsonage and its attached lands (the glebe), the right to the tithes, and the ownership of other dues. The benefice could, however, become divorced from the holder of the office if the advowson (or patronage) belonged to a monastery or cathedral, as the institution could decide to keep the income itself, and hire a vicar (or substitute) to perform spiritual duties. (This might occur for funding the central monastery, but was clearly done in some cases to finance major reconstruction or re-organisation of the local parish.)

This power to appropriate the rectorial income of a parish was originally restricted to religious owners, probably as a practical means of allowing some flexibility in arranging church affairs. When the rights and resources of these institutions were seized in the 1530s, however, they were redistributed to the lay population as well as to the cathedrals, and the right of receiving the income could be retained by a "lay rector" who employed his own vicar.

(To clarify the third term applied to priests - a curate - all priests having responsibility for the "cure" of souls within a parish are technically curates. In England, however, the term is usually applied to a person hired by the rector or vicar as an assistant; in the case of lay rectors, who cannot themselves have the cure of souls, the curate and vicar are one and the same.)

The most obvious effect of patronage was surely the practice of younger sons of landed families becoming priests in order to be presented with the local rectorship. This had the dual benefit of providing younger sons with an income (or sons-in-law, as part of a dowry settlement), while retaining control of the land within the family. It underlines the fact that livings, in the Marsh as elsewhere, were valuable pieces of property which could be bought, sold and leased in the same way as any other part of one's estate.

"Gentry incumbents" were perhaps less significant in Romney Marsh than elsewhere, as the advowsons of many marsh churches were long owned by either the abbey or the cathedral at Canterbury. Prior to the Dissolution, no fewer than 14 of the 18 churches covered by this guide were held by the Archbishop or a religious establishment - an abbey, priory, hospital, or college which had been given them at some date - with the only exceptions being the livings of Bilsington (privately-owned before it was given in 1253 to the newly-founded Priory), Old Romney, Rye and East Guldeford. (The last was truly an exception, however, as it was not founded until c. 1500 and was thus always privately owned.)

The situation changed after monastic lands were parcelled out by Henry VIII, when the division became 10 religious patrons and 8 private ones. There were, however, some oddities: the advowsons of Burmarsh and Dymchurch were privately owned, but by the Crown; that of Fairfield, while owned by the Dean and Chapter of Canterbury, was leased out with the local manor to private owners.

Certainly those advowsons in Romney Marsh which were privately held show the same use of "family rectors" as found elsewhere. Bonnington, for example, was owned in the early 1700s by the Turner family, and the living was given to family rectors. It was sold c.1780 to David Papillon, who had married into the Turner family; he carried on the tradition by presenting Philip Papillon to the living in 1785. At Brenzett, the Rev. R.D. Brockman owned the patronage of his own living in the early 1800s, and other examples of advowsons being owned by the rector can be found at East Guldeford, Hope and Hurst.

These ancient rights of nomination remained largely untouched until the turn of the century. Since then, however, they have been so severely circumscribed that any remaining privately-owned advowsons are now largely ceremonial. Changes began in 1898, with a requirement to register all transfers of the right of presentation with the Bishop. Clergy who owned the right of presentation were banned from presenting themselves in 1923; diocesan Boards of Patronage were established in 1932; and the payment of tithes directly to parish priests was finally abolished in 1936. A provision of 1923 eventually made rights of presentation unsaleable unless they were legally appendant to the ownership of a manor or land; and from 1968 the Bishop had the power to suspend the right of presentation for successive periods of up to five years. Finally, in 1986, all advowsons appendant to land or manorial ownership were severed for legal purposes, thus marking the formal end to a linkage which had its roots in the earliest foundation of Christian parishes in England.

CIVIL PARISHES

The civil parish, represented locally by the "parish vestry", is an ancient form of local government which developed out of the decline and decay of the feudal system of manorial courts. The latter was a very decentralised system, and was thus particularly suited to an often-beseiged, agricultural society.

As outlined in the introduction, the basic system also predates Christianity. When Christian parish churches came to be established - that is, after about 700 A.D. - most occupied or settled lands in the country were already held under seigneurial lordships. By the very nature of a feudal system, all settled or cultivated land was already under someone's control. Newly cultivated and/or settled land similarly came under the complete control of a thane - whether that happened to be an individual or an institution such as a monastery - and it is this factor which accounts for the need for some sort of agreement to be made to found the parish church and endow a rectorship. The fact that all of the populated land of the country was held by a feudal owner led logically to Archbishop Theodore's dioceses being based upon the kingdoms of the land, subdivided along feudal tribe boundaries.

Since manors provided the original setting into which many ancient parish churches were fitted - and later formed the basis for the area controlled by the parish vestry - an understanding of the nature of a fiefdom will help to clarify the eventual development of parish government.

St Mary, East Guldeford

At base, a manor is a set of rights rather than a specific location: it consists of a number of rights vested in the lord, including both rights in respect of lands and certain rights of jurisdiction over tenants. Within the manor, two types of lands existed: demesne lands, and tenemental lands.

Demesne lands were those which were owned freehold by the lord. They included his own land - whether occupied personally or leased to a "customary tenant" for a set number of years - as well as the waste land. The latter, of course, was usually subject to rights of common by all tenants, regardless of their particular status.

Tenemental lands were those held by "freehold tenants". Unlike fixed-term (or customary) tenants, they held their property by virtue of certain services and for payments provided to the lord. The lands were freehold in the sense that they could be sold or bequeathed by the tenant, in whole or in part, and without the lord's consent, as long as the requisite services or payments were fulfilled. It was essential for the existence of a manor that there should be freehold tenants, as these had to sit as the manorial "court baron". (In actual fact there had to be at least two freehold tenants, as a court could not be held with just one.)

Rather than being an invidious system of serfdom, this was an accepted and extremely efficient system of controlling the nation, based on the heirarchical order of service by the freehold tenant to his lord, who in turn held his manor by service to a superior manor or to the king himself. The service in many cases was payment; it could take any form, however, and in an age when private feudal armies were an essential security precaution, it often took the form of knight's service.

This requirement of service in return for land holdings was in fact too efficient, and as centralised government became more sophisticated it eventually began to threaten the stability of the nation. In this context, two dates are critical: 1215, when by Magna Carta the great barons (landed lords who owed services only to the king) forced king John to recognise their power; and 1289, the year in which Edward I and the barons banned the creation of new freehold tenancies held by services owed to their sub-lords (known as "subinfeudination"). This was arguably the greatest change ever made to the structure of land ownership in this country: it fixed forever the existing manors, blocked the creation of new fiefdoms, and thus set in motion the death of feudal land tenure. Ancient parishes were, however, well established by this date, and as the manorial courts died out over the centuries, the parish became its natural successor as a unit of local government.

Manorial courts generally died out in the 1500s and 1600s, but had really been overtaken by parishes by the 1550s. (More isolated areas kept the courts active for another two hundred years or so, and the feudal system was not formally wound up until 1926, when all outstanding customary tenancies were converted by statute to freeholdings.)

Basic government in the parish was exercised by the vestry - an open meeting rooted in Anglo-Saxon "folk gemots", a system of government still practised in rural Switzerland. It was this body which gradually took over most of the powers of manorial courts in respect of parish upkeep and administration. The switch from manorial officials to their parochial equivalents was, however, gradual and relatively seamless. Two of the principal parish officers were direct descendants of earlier officials:

the manorial "tythingman", responsible for the good government of the manor, became the parish constable, while church wardens - originally ecclesiastical officers - retained their role of protecting and repairing the parish church and took on the role of administering the church rate levied for this purpose by the parish vestry.

By the 1550s, this replacement system had developed sufficiently for the vestries - a word which first appears in this context in 1507 - to be charged by statute with the upkeep of highways. This involved the establishment of a new parish officer, the surveyor, responsible for the roads as well as for supervising statutory labour. (The latter is interesting: from the 16th century until 1835, all adults within a parish were required to contribute six days' labour per annum - or the equivalent in wages, often used to employ the poor - towards the upkeep of local roads.) In 1601, the vestries were officially given their major role of poor relief, a role which lasted for well over 200 years until the Poor Acts of the 1830s.

The provision of poor relief dramatically underlines the common roots of civil and ecclesiastical parishes. Originally, it appears that even the rector's tithes were in fact meant to be held in trust to support the poor; only later did they come to be seen as the rector's personal property. Poor relief then fell to charitable bequests from parochial inhabitants, fulfilling the common law requirement that the poor were to be sustained by parsons, rectors of the church, and parishioners, "so that none should die for default of sustenance". It was only after this common-law system failed in the late 1500s - to a great extent due to the nationalisation in the 1530s of the great wealth of the monasteries, including their charities - that the parish vestries were formally charged with the relief of the poor, and given the right to levy a rate for this purpose.

Vestries reached their peak of power in terms of local government in the period between the Poor Acts of 1601 and those of the 1830s. They were never abolished, of course, but all of their important powers were transferred bit by bit to other statutory bodies. Poor relief was removed in 1834; highway maintenance in the 1830s and 1860s; policing and lighting of streets in the 1830s and 1840s; and health services in the 1840s and 1870s. Their remaining civil responsibilities were transferred in 1894 to the new parish councils, and even the remnant responsibility for the parish church was given to Parochial Church Councils in the early 1920s. These later refinements of parish government are, however, only of peripheral concern as far as church building and embellishment are concerned.

THE MARSH AND ITS OWNERS

It is not the aim of this work to detail the history of the Marsh; interested readers will no doubt be familiar with the general history, or will follow up any specific points of interest. On the other hand, if the marsh churches are to be placed in a wider context, some idea of the peculiar nature of the Marsh is called for, along with a grasp of the chronology of draining the marshes, the creation of social institutions, etc. It was within this context that church buildings developed.

To understand the Marsh's church builders and churches, one must begin with the Marsh itself, its strangeness, and its attraction - all of which are rooted in the relation with the sea. The very word "marsh" embodies this ambiguous split between the sea and the land - it comes from a word meaning "sea-" or "lake-ish" - and the "water-ish" nature has always cut both ways. While it meant that the natural vegetation was eminently suited for grazing animals (cattle were sent here for a sort of curative treatment), it was always a difficult and unhealthy place for man. A huge swamp, sometimes part of the sea, and sometimes land, its islands and peninsulas were always at the mercy of the water for their shape and even their very existence.

From the first, of course, the land of the marsh was manipulated by man; it was not a place where nature was simply allowed to take its course. The Rhee "wall", now known to be a medieval waterway constructed c.1200 to replace the rapidly-shifting course of the Rother, is obviously an early attempt to combat the fickle nature of the area's drainage. The new line also established the division between the Romney and Walland Marshes - the former, to the east, being the longer-occupied lands, with the inning of the latter not starting until well after the Norman conquest. The water also dictated the density of settlement, and set up the age-old split between the Portsmen (residents of the Cinque Ports) and the Marshemen (who lived out in the marsh itself).

The Marsh was thus inned (or drained) over a period of centuries, and activity - particularly in the "new" areas of Walland Marsh - seems predictably to have increased after the Conquest. The population was never great, though: in a marsh zone, farming demands proportionately more land to gain an equivalent yield than would be the case for more fertile holdings, and low population figures are one of the few historical constants of the Marsh. In Romney Marsh, these natural problems were exacerbated by the proximity of the Channel. It was always the entry point for continental raids and invasions, and early mediaeval settlement here was founded on a fragile political base as well as physically shifting sands.

Natural demands led to the co-operative system of the Lords of Romney Marsh, responsible from ancient times for the maintenance of the sea defences. Defence from human opponents, however, can be dated to the development of the mediaeval Cinque Ports as a confederation which supplied the king with ships and men for the defence of the coast and the channel. (Although in existence from the mid 1100s, the confederation was formalised in 1278; significant privileges were granted in return for the assured provision of manned ships from those who had long mastered the sea.)

It was this same threat which undoubtedly contributed, along with the Black Death, to the depopulation of Romney Marsh in the late 1300s. This was the first half of the Hundred Years

War, when increased French raids were added to the natural harshness of life on the marsh. By early 1462, the marsh had become so unattractive a place that Edward IV - on the throne for less than a year - thought it expedient to grant the Marsh the privileges of a Liberty. Edward's charter itself states that the main reason for granting these rights was to encourage people to settle in this vulnerable corner of the kingdom, and the date of the charter (early 1462) is telling. In March 1461, Edward had ascended the throne as the Yorkist successor to Henry VI, and Henry, of course, had been king of both England and France. His loss of the latter was a contributing factor to the Wars of the Roses and to his eventual downfall, but Henry remained a threat to Edward: given the former king's connections, it is hardly surprising to find that Edward was worried about a French invasion. (The point was proved when Henry was briefly restored to the throne in 1471.)

The charter for this new Liberty was astonishingly generous, underlining the urgent need for settlement; indeed, it set up a virtual free state within the kingdom, subject largely to its own laws and to some of the king's.

Ruled by a bailiff, 24 jurats, and the "communalty" of the Marsh - the latter being the new civic corporation - the new body chose its own Justices; held a court every three weeks to hear all pleas - personal and real, civil and criminal - and was free of any jurisdiction of justices, commissioners or sheriffs within the county of Kent. It received the benefit of all fines, writs, forfeits, etc., including all penalties judged against marsh residents - regardless of where those judgements were given; claimed all local wrecks, forfeited property, attained estates, etc., again regardless of where judgement was given; executed judgements, including capital punishment, as decreed by the court of the Liberty; and could levy taxes and enforce ordinances for good local government. Residents of the marsh were to be exempt from all taxes, including tolls for land and sea passage throughout England, as well as from any charges for access to markets and fairs throughout the country; to be exempt from any special taxes granted by Parliament to the king, even if the local representatives themselves voted for the tax; and, finally, to be excused from serving on juries or assizes dealing with matters outside of the marsh boundaries, as well as from all of the other normal requirements for personal service demanded of other citizens of the land. These remarkable rights, however, were strictly limited to the area east of the Rhee channel. They did not extend to the Walland or Denge Marshes, nor to the soon-to-be-inned area of the East Guldeford Level. This created two types of community within the larger area usually called "Romney Marsh", and even today a glance at the Ordnance Survey shows a distinct difference between the two: the area to the east has been settled with a regular and dense pattern of roads and villages, while the Walland and Denge marshes are largely devoted to pastureland.

Admittedly, this division between the two areas was an ancient one, based on the early occupation of the areas to the east. Of the seventeen churches dealt with in this guide which predate Edward's charter of 1462 (recalling that East Guldeford was a later foundation), only four lay outside of the liberty's side of the dividing line. Two of these - Lydd and Rye - served large ancient towns, leaving only the two churches of Fairfield and Brookland falling outside of the liberty before the latter was established by the charter of 1462. Even given this ancient division, however, the differences between the two zones are striking, and their continued survival into modern times must surely reflect to some degree the generous privileges which were accorded the residents of the liberty.

One aspect of life on the marshes which no number of royal decrees could change was the fact that geographically the entire marsh belonged more to the sea than to the heights of land which surround it: for many centuries the level of the sea has been rising in relation to the south of England. Whether the land is sinking, or the sea is rising, may be in some dispute; the effect has, however, been the same, and for centuries the people of the marsh have had to fight against - or at least try to compensate for - the shifting line between what is land and what is sea.

All too often it was a losing battle. An entire island was submerged in 1087, creating the Goodwin Sands, and severe storms in the middle and late 1200s were even worse. Winchelsea was so devastated by storms of the 1250s - half the town of 700 houses was destroyed - that 30 years later Edward I abandoned the rapidly-disappearing site and laid out a new town on the heights to the west of the old. Even more serious, as it affected the fortunes of a greater number of towns, was the change in the course of the Rother. This left New Romney without its port; eventually shifted the main mouth of the river to Rye; and indirectly allowed the drainage of the rest of Walland Marsh and the East Guldeford Level.

The fortunes of the people of the marsh were thus directly linked to the sea - not only in the sense of providing harbours, wrecks, and the marsh's notorious opportunities for smuggling, but

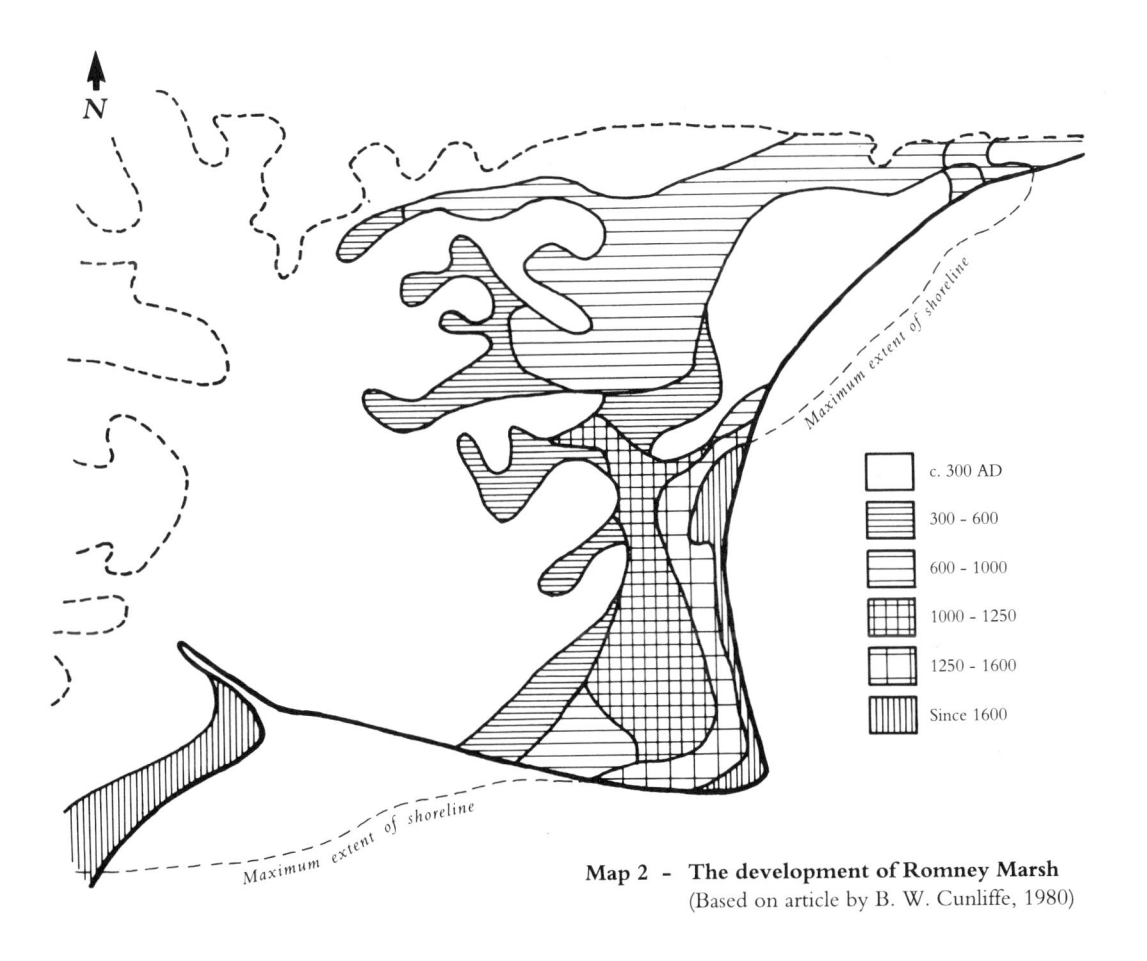

Map 2 - The development of Romney Marsh
(Based on article by B. W. Cunliffe, 1980)

also by physically giving and taking away land. The churches are the physical embodiment of this long-gone society - a culture which, when it erected a church, was not primarily concerned with aesthetics, nor indeed solely with religion as we tend to think of it today, as the buildings were a part of every aspect of the organisation, economy and running of the area and, indeed, the nation. The marsh, and the age to which the churches date, dictated social organisation; the society - both economic and religious - produced the landowners; and the landowners (or gentry) by and large produced the churches.

Land and property rights were the source of mediaeval wealth, political power, military power, and thus social standing. Such rights were jealously guarded by their owners, and protected where necessary by law. It is extremely significant that for some 200 years the laws of primogeniture involved more than just the passing of an estate to the first-born: from 1285, a legal prohibition was also included on the sale of any part of an "entailed" estate in order to protect it for the future heir. (This led to all sorts of problems, along with the requirement for licences from the Crown to alienate, and the legal difficulties were not resolved until the late 1400s. Indeed, until 1540 it was not legally possible to will land - other than for life terms or other legal interests - to anyone other than the first-born.)

To give a brief - if somewhat complex - example of how estates were kept and used within families, let us look at a series of intermarriages which involved no less than eleven of the twenty-three Lordships of Romney Marsh over a period of some 500 years.

In the late 1530s, Jane Hawte (or Haut) married Sir Thomas Wyatt, an influential member of Henry VIII's court. The new Lady Wyatt brought to Sir Thomas her family's manor of Blackmanstone (held since c.1350), Snave (since at least 1475), and Warehorne. The latter had come to the Hawte family via a similar route of marriage to the family of Peckham; in turn, the Peckham family had obtained it by marriage with the de Maraunts, the owners from the mid 1300s.

Under 16th-century law, of course, Sir Thomas and not his wife owned the estates. In 1541, he exchanged two of them (Blackmanstone and Snave) with the Crown for other properties; his wife's third dowry estate of Warehorne, however, passed to the Twysden family when one of the Wyatts' daughters married Roger Twysden. It is clear what is happening here. Warehorne acted as a dowry estate for, at the very least, four separate marriages. Some changes were made by the Twysdens (Honychild was sold by them in the 1500s), but Warehorne and Eastbridge remained with the family until the 1700s when they both passed to the Dering family in a marriage agreement. The Derings then bolstered their local holdings with Tinton and Burmarsh manors; they also purchased Honychild, thus retrieving a former family property.

While this was going on, Eastwell Manor had long belonged to the Finch family (the Earls of Winchelsea and Nottingham), and Burmarsh had belonged to them in the 1500s. Like the ownership of Warehorne, Eastwell had come to the Finches through a marriage with the Moyle family (owners of Packmanstone, Kenardington and Bonnington). In terms of mediaeval society, however, it is no coincidence that the Finches and the Twysdens were linked by marriage: Anne Finch, the granddaughter of the Moyle heiress, married Sir William Twysden – Sir Thomas Wyatt's grandson, whose descendants eventually took Warehorne to the Derings.

In themselves, these connections are not particularly important, and were duplicated all over the country. They do, however, show the extent to which any exploration of one family or one manor leads to other families and linked holdings. One seldom finds families with just one manor, and it is here, at the level of the smaller holdings of the gentry, that the most important level of local government lay for most of the country's population. It is also here – where achievements are measured in knighthoods and baronetcies rather than chancellorships and earldoms – that one finds the bulk of the contributors to smaller parish churches. It is their embellishments that have created our churches, and it is in an attempt to place this development in context for each church that the second half of this book has been written.

St Thomas-a-Becket, Fairfield

CHURCHES AND CHANGE

It should by now be clear that the general form of parish churches was dictated firstly by liturgical needs, while much of the lasting form reflects the embellishments of owners and parishoners rather than the stylistic fashions of architecture which happened to be current at any given date.

In terms of the usual approach of architectural history, this view is no doubt seen as perverse. One can, however, argue very strongly that architectural styles are principally interesting for dating features of buildings; except in a narrow technical sense dealing with the development of structure, they have very little inherent interest. It should never be forgotten that the architecture was simply a means: the religious use of the building was the ultimate point of the whole exercise.

In terms of liturgical needs, it is useful to understand the nature of a mediaeval church as opposed to churches which were adapted for completely different liturgies after the Reformation. As pointed out by Addleshaw and Etchells in their work on the architectural setting of Anglican worship, the plan of an English mediaeval parish church was a result of combining a series of compartments within a single building. The nave, the aisles, the chantry chapels, the chancels and their aisles separated from the nave by a screen, rood-loft and typanum - all of these housed quite distinct and separate functions. The Renaissance and post-Reformation view of these various "rooms" being subordinate to a greater, comprehensive spacial design was quite alien to the mediaeval concept of a church. Two examples should suffice to elaborate this point: the issue of vistas from the nave to the high altar, and the function of aisles.

The division in a church had originally been twofold: a sanctuary in which the altar was placed, and a nave where the faithful could assemble and where a choir could be accommodated. It was not a building designed for the communal worship of large numbers - even in large towns, the Middle Ages preferred numerous small churches to a few large ones - let alone communal worship by the laity and clergy. Clerical functions occurred at the east, beyond the screen; the laity worshipped in the nave; embellishments such as chantry chapels, side altars and votary lights were housed in the aisles; no need was seen for any visible spacial linkage between the various functions.

It was not until the Reformation's demand for more communal worship, followed by the Victorian reordering of churches to reflect what was perceived as pre-Reformation practice, that the idea of an unbroken vista from the back of a long church to the high altar became fashionable. (Indeed, it has often been pointed out that the creation of such a vista in mediaeval cathedrals in fact subverts the original proportions of such buildings' individual "rooms".)

A similar misapprehension can be seen in the modern concept of aisles. Aisles were not introduced into mediaeval churches to provide parallel corridors to the nave: they were meant primarily to house side altars and small chapels, accessed through the nave arcade and divided from one another by screens. Again, it was the post-Reformation removal of such catholic practices as chantries, and the substitution of preaching-based, communal liturgies, which led to aisles being adapted for new uses such as additional seating.

Aside from liturgical demands, the most potent force which shaped the form of individual churches was, of course, that of the patrons and parishoners. The marsh churches provide many examples of patronage by the owners of manors and of the rights of presentation. Bilsington, for example, had been served from the 1250s to the 1530s by the local Priory; after the Dissolution, the church was granted to Anthony St. Leger, and then sold in the 1560s to Francis Barnham. Barnham's son (later knighted) found it to be long neglected, and repaired the building in 1590 - less than 25 years after his father had bought the manor. The estate then stayed in the family for at least 200 years, but the eventual passing of ownership to another family did not change the nature of repair and embellishment: the lord of the manor in the early 1900s, R.J. Balston, was honoured with a memorial window in 1916, and one of his successors, the Hon. Mr. Justice Luxmoore, donated a reredos as a memorial to his two sons (both of whom were killed in the second World War).

Some of the churches, of course, show less direct involvement of owners than do others, and particularly in the case of larger towns the embellishments tended to be by notable parishioners rather than owners. At Rye, for example, a chantry chapel was endowed in the 1280s, and the "Lamb vault" - a family tomb - may also reflect a chantry endowment. Similarly, in the present century two stained glass windows were donated to Rye by E.F. Benson, the novelist and son of Archbishop Benson, along with the Archbishop's chalice dating to 1690.

Most of the marsh's churches - even large buildings such as Lydd and Ivychurch - are more-or-less "normal" parish churches, with their ancient ownerships and congregations being reflected by rebuildings, embellishments, memorial stones, and bequests. Bequests were, of course, much more important prior to the Dissolution and to the 17th-century Puritan cleansing of churches: almost all of the churches record legacies left for the lighting of candles, the saying of masses, etc., before such votary bequests fell out of fashion.

Thus, most churches had local roles to play - some are traditionally held to have been pilgrimage stops, for example - but at least two must be viewed as being substantially different. Horne chapel, now

St Mary, Rye

owned by English Heritage, was a private chapel associated with a manor house, and is not dealt with in detail in this guide. East Guldeford was similarly a private foundation, in that the entire parish was reclaimed from the marsh, starting in the late 1400s, and the parish church was erected between 1499 and 1505. Both of these churches should show a different history of development to that of the ancient parish churches of the marsh.

The important point to make here is that until about a century ago, churches were generally viewed and treated simply as buildings designed to house religious observance. For spiritual reasons, these buildings were constructed as fine pieces of architecture; nevertheless, they were still working buildings, not works of architecture which just happened to house church services - a view which is often inherent today in modern architectural history books and church guides.

Our culture usually approaches a church in one of two ways (sometimes combining elements of both): either a physical "tour" is made of the building, starting from the entrance, or the history is given in terms of architectural features, followed by memorials and other embellishments. This may be convenient, but creates a false impression: no church has ever developed in a clockwise direction starting from the south door, nor as a group of arches, followed by a group of doorcases, followed by a number of memorials.

This modern approach dates to the 19th century, but became common practice only in the 20th. The reasons for it are complex, and do not warrant examination here; suffice it to say that neither a "physical tour" approach, nor a study of architectural features adequately explains to a casual visitor how a church has developed.

The best way to understand a church's development in the context of its society is to take quite a strict chronological approach. This puts the main focus upon the forces which created the church, rather than upon the ultimate form which those forces took. In national terms, the main forces were liturgical and political; locally, they tended to be physical - especially in Romney Marsh - or social (the wealth of the parish, and/or the presence of individual benefactors).

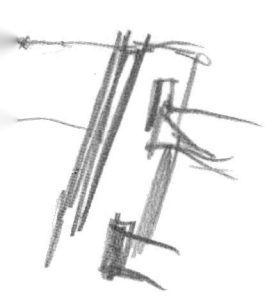

Stylistically, national trends in church design seem to run in 100-year cycles - admittedly something of a simplification, but related to technical advances such as the pointed arch, and practically useful as an aide-memoire for casual visitors to parish churches.

Generally speaking, the Normans rebuilt Saxon churches in stone during the 1100s, and added aisles and towers in the 1200s. During the 1300s and 1400s, pious embellishments such as windows, rood screens and other fixtures were added, and the 1500s were concerned with the Reformation and the Puritan cleansing of churches (including the removal of ancient stone altars and the previous century's rood screens). The early 1600s saw the blossoming of preaching and the destruction of graven images; while the late 1600s and 1700s saw the development of a more secular church which turned the use of private box pews into a fine art and introduced high pulpits and galleries to allow the priest to see the entire congregation.

In the 1800s the church underwent an extremely vigorous religious revival, and the inward-looking pews of the previous century - where an entire family could meet together, with some having their backs to the preacher - were re-arranged so that the entire congregation faced the high altar. Our own time has seen a move away from formal forms of worship, and has once more introduced significant changes to the physical layout of churches.

These changes affect both the buildings themselves and the way we look at them. In terms of the 20th century's art-based approach, for example, one of the most unfortunate periods has long been considered to be the 19th century: almost all of the eighteen churches dealt with by this book underwent Victorian "restorations" to a greater or lesser extent, and much physical evidence of the history of the churches was lost.

It is accepted practice to damn these restorations, and they did undoubtedly remove some of the continuity of embellishment which makes buildings interesting in architectural and human terms. Nevertheless, the Victorian restorations must be viewed in light of changing demands, and should not merely be damned out of hand for the very real destruction of historical features which resulted from the changes.

The late 17th and 18th centuries may not have been as philistine as the Victorians claimed, but could never be portrayed as a period of great piousness in the English church: it was a time of absentee and gentleman rectors, poorly-paid curates and, more often than not, weak bishops. This secular nature was, of course, partly a reaction to the excesses of 17th-century Puritanism, and found its physical expression in private pews, galleries for the less well-off, and the order (of 1660) that each church was to display the royal coat of arms. This re-assertion of royal supremacy at the Restoration seems somehow perfectly to capture the tone of the English church in the age of reason, an age which lasted for about 150 years and became quite entrenched. (It took a formal order of 1808, for example, to force even as admired a churchman as Sydney Smith to reside in the parish from which he took his living).

Predictably, there followed a period of great renewal in the church, and the clearance of elements of the "secular church" - such as box pews, where some of the congregation might face the rear of the church, and the lower-class gallery seats - would have been seen as a sign of a revitalised church casting off some of the more sordid practices of its immediate predecessors.

Like the changes of the 16th, 17th and 18th centuries, this reaction was zealous and insensitive. Old buildings were purged of all their history, often back to the bare stones of the church or further, and it took admirable new groups such as the Society for the Protection of Ancient Buildings (known to one of its founders, William Morris, as "anti-scrape") to point out that change did not necessarily have to mean the elimination of all traces of history. It is, however, every bit as important to recognize the forces behind the Victorian work as it is to understand the alterations of the 16th century, and what is now viewed as an excess of zeal should not be taken in any way to diminish the vitality of the underlying religious renewal of the 19th century.

These general changes were the result of national movements which affected all parish churches; let us never forget, however, that individual churches are also the result of local forces, and that even a local grouping such as "churches of Romney Marsh" will hide a wide variation in individual buildings.

Probably the most prevalent image of a marsh church is that epitomised by Fairfield - a lonesome, isolated building which seems to mark the site of some past settlement or place of pilgrimage, but which has for centuries been at the mercy of the marsh's subsidence and floods. In reality each church has a distinct history - Fairfield seems to have been founded when the marsh was inned, possibly in the hope of a population which never arrived - and even within the marsh there were at least three distinct types of churches: town churches (Dymchurch, New Romney, Lydd and Rye); those like Bilsington and Bonnington, which overlook the marsh from the heights above the Royal Military Canal; and the "classic", isolated marsh churches such as Fairfield and St. Mary-in-the-Marsh. (Not suprisingly, the town churches tend to be the grandest, while the marsh churches best evoke the history of pilgrims, the sea, and smugglers. The "edge of marsh" churches, on the other hand, tend to have lovely pastoral settings and the best views.)

To some extent, however, even these groupings are specious, as the differences are at least as important as the similarities. Every church has its own particular history, and similarities should never be emphasised at the expense of the history and dignity embodied in their differences. Dymchurch and Old Romney, for example, are both ancient marsh churches, but differ entirely in terms of continuity: the former was a very poor parish, and the building shows this; the latter was clearly well-funded throughout its life and contains an astonishingly complete record of its embellishment. Similarly, while many of the churches show obvious evidence of subsidence - there are many massive buttresses, crooked towers, rebuilt walls and leaning arcades - each found a different solution. At Newchurch, the tower was begun, left to settle, and finished later, apparently after some administrative re-organisation which involved re-endowing the perpetual vicarage. At the tiny church of All Saints, Burmarsh, however, it appears that when the nave collapsed it was simply rebuilt with a roof lower than that of the chancel.

The importance of looking at the particular context of each church cannot be overstressed: for example, many of the marsh churches have architectural details of the late 1300s, and Ivychurch may seem to be just a particularly grand example of the period. When one looks at the size, details and context, however, it becomes notably clear that Ivychurch is unique among the marsh's churches in that it was re-founded and even re-dedicated during the hundred Years' War - probably combining a pious offering with visible reassurance of the population, and giving a building which was battlemented and large enough to act as a communal stronghold.

Readers of this book are encouraged to purchase the small guides which can be obtained for a small donation at each church, and which list important monuments, legatees, architectural features, and rectors. The following descriptions of the churches do not attempt to repeat this information in detail; they are, however, meant to be more than just an evocative description of each church's sense of place. Each description provides a chronological account which tries to shed light on how the building developed over time, with physical changes being made to accommodate new practices or circumstances, and memorials being added or removed as congregations and patrons came and left. It is hoped that this will help to explain some of the forces which created each church as an individual and lasting monument to the people of the parishes and to the ever-present influence of the marsh.

THE CHURCHES

St Augustine, Snave

ST. PETER AND ST. PAUL
BILSINGTON

A church - presumably a simple wooden structure - existed at Bilsington by Domesday, but was rebuilt in stone within about a century after the Conquest. This may have reflected the ruination of the old church, or a desire by the Normans to remove evidence of their Saxon predecessors. An additional factor could have been the increased practice of pilgrimages to Canterbury after Becket's death in 1170, as it would have meant an increased demand for more substantial church buildings throughout Kent.

Bilsington saw fairly constant embellishment and change over the next 200 years: the chancel arch, usually a somewhat mean feature in Norman churches, was enlarged to its present impressive size in the early 1200s; the north side nave windows were inserted in the 1300s; and the lancet windows in the north and south sides of the chancel were added in the 1400s. Gifts to the church included the 15th-century bell from a London bell-founder, John Jordan - now in the churchyard, as its 900-pound weight was too much for the bell tower - and, perhaps, the mediaeval font.

This was the period during which the church was owned by Bilsington Priory, the advowson and income having been given by Roger de Somery, along with the manor of Bilsington Superior, when the priory was founded in 1253. (Bilsington Inferior kept the manor-house. The terms "superior" and "inferior", it should be noted, were simply descriptive: Bilsington Superior covered the high ground, while Inferior referred to the lower marsh lands. The terms did not imply any relative status between the two manors.)

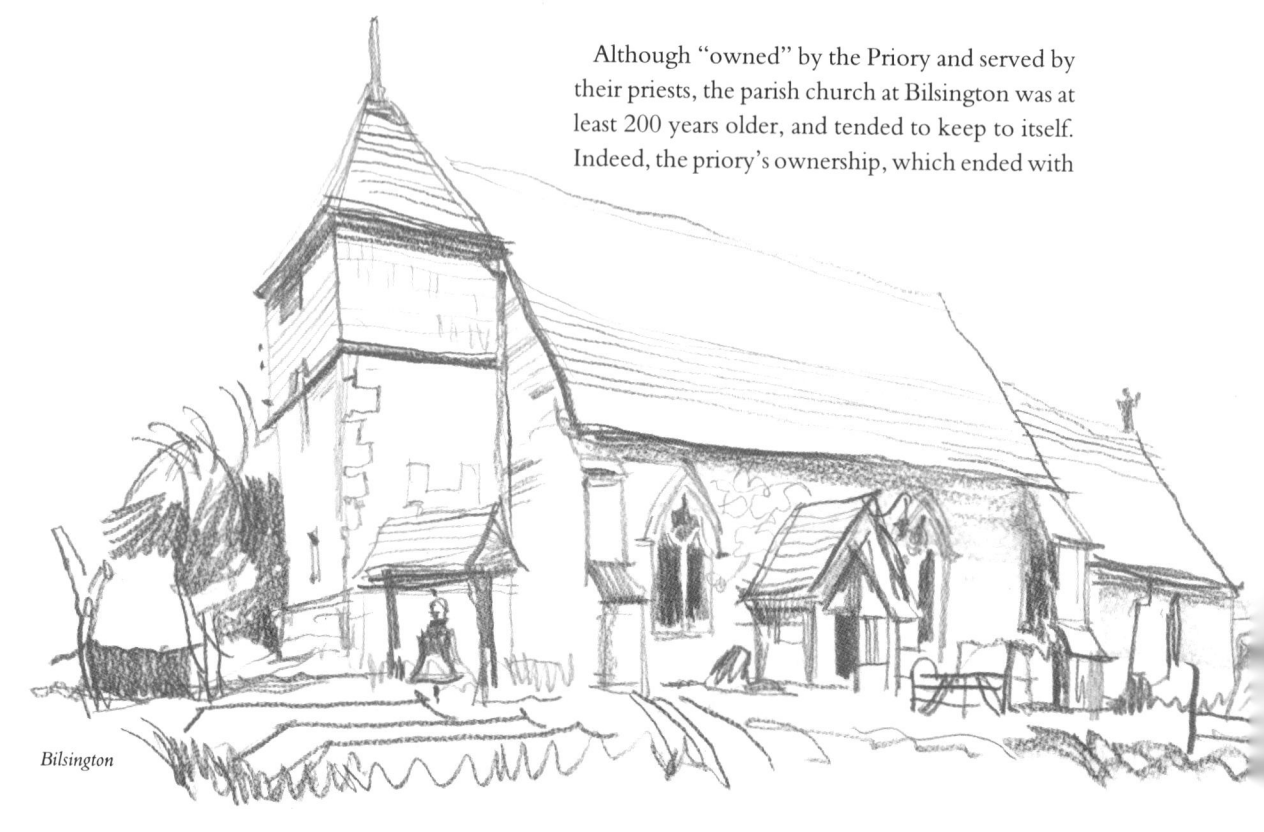

Although "owned" by the Priory and served by their priests, the parish church at Bilsington was at least 200 years older, and tended to keep to itself. Indeed, the priory's ownership, which ended with

Bilsington

the Dissolution, can be considered as little more than a 300-year episode of the church's 900-plus years of history, equivalent to the ownership from the 1560s to the early 1800s by the Barnham and Rider families.

Certainly, embellishment of the parish church seems to have continued almost independently of the priory - there is evidence of various doors and windows being blocked and opened, reflecting the normal life of a working building - and the running-down of the religious houses meant that the fabric of the church suffered rather than benefited from being the priory's responsibility. When local parish life - never extinguished - again took control in the 1500s, neglect had taken its toll. By 1590 the church was in need of major repairs, financed by the then-lord of the manor, Martin Barnham of Hollingbourne. It was probably not long after this time that, in common with most churches, private pews began to become common - an innovation which eventually led to a gallery being inserted at the west end to accommodate the less wealthy.

As mentioned in the introduction, the order in 1660 to display royal coats of arms in the churches reasserted royal supremacy. Bilsington's arms are a particularly pleasing example: dated 1774, and showing the arms of George III, they were painted by Joseph Gibson of Woodchurch.

Like many rural churches, Bilsington avoided the attention of Victorian improvers for longer than many, remaining in its unchanged form until as late as 1883. The eventual restoration, under the vicar F. Martin Cameron and by the architect Joseph Clarke, involved the removal of the roof kingposts, box pews, west-end gallery, pulpit, and an ancient organ, and extension of the chancel by adding a new sanctuary. A wooden-framed, stained glass window which had replaced the three original Norman lights at the east end was also removed, and replaced by the existing round-headed, Norman windows. (The existing stained glass in these windows was added as a memorial to Richard James Balston, the lay rector of the church who restored Bilsington Priory and died in 1916.)

The work at Bilsington was admittedly drastic, and it is always disappointing to think that physical reminders of the past have been irrevocably lost by modern restorers who should, frankly, have known better. Nevertheless, and cold comfort though it may be, the work of 1883 was probably more sensitively carried out than if it had been started 40 years earlier. Also, crudely put, it made room for modern memorials to take their place. Aside from the east-end windows, mentioned above, gifts during the present century have included the pulpit (1915, from the lay rector R.J. Balston); the reredos (dedicated by the Archbishop of Canterbury in 1942 as a memorial to the family of Justice Luxmoore, both of whose sons were killed in the second World War); and other memorials such as the window to the Rev. R.G. Cooper (1955) and the font cover (1956, in memory of Hannah Edmunds, a teacher in the Sunday School).

These new embellishments are, of course, not as inherently appealing to outside eyes as would be their ancient equivalents, and they would undoubtedly have gained an historical context by sitting next to older memorials. They do, however, continue the practice of decorating churches by parishioners and the private owners of an advowson, and add their own continuity to this small, ancient church which still shows so much evidence of its 700 years overlooking the marsh.

ST. RUMWOLD
BONNINGTON

This small, isolated church, overlooking the Royal Military Canal, is often more remarked upon for its dedication – an exceedingly rare one – than for the qualities of the building itself. The building is more complex than it seems, however, and admirably displays its development over time.

A church is listed here at Domesday, and the dedication to St. Rumwold suggests a Saxon foundation of the 7th or 8th century. (The saint's legend is that of a child born in King's Sutton to a pagan father and Christian mother; he proclaimed his religion upon coming out of the womb; preached on his second day of life, specifying his own name; and died on the third.)

The little Saxon church, dedicated to the equally little Saxon saint, was rebuilt by the Normans, who presumably supplied the existing font. The manor of Bonnington, along with the advowson of the church, was then given by the Crown to the Knights Hospitallers of St. John of Jerusalem (founded at London c.1144), who kept it until their Dissolution in 1540.

The Hospitallers tended to the church, rebuilding and reroofing the nave in the 1300s – the date of the nave windows as well as the chancel arch. By and large, however, the peaceful and isolated little church would have remained unchanged until it was given away in 1542.

For some 40 years after the Dissolution, the advowson of the church and the ownership of the local manor were split apart. It may be this period to which the Perpendicular timber porch dates, although the feature may have been added during the course of the 1400s. In any event, major changes were not made until the advowson passed, as part of a marriage settlement

Bonnington

in about 1580, to Sir James Hales, the owner of Bonnington Manor.

Hales and his descendants retained control of the church and manor until the middle of the 17th-century, and it is to this period that the distinctive turret and cupola, the remnant of the west end gallery, and the font cover date. As was the case with most small churches, the gallery was probably inserted for liturgical reasons, and to provide seating which was progressively appropriated by privately-owned box pews.

18th-century alterations again reflected the changing needs and tone of the church in general. The very fine pulpit dates to this century - during which the advowson and manor were leased to the Turner family and then sold (in 1780) to the Papillon family - as does the royal coat of arms placed prominently above the chancel arch.

The sense of order which characterises 18th-century life - and, indeed, 18th-century design in general - is well reflected by these two elements of church furnishing and their positioning in relation to the older features of St. Rumwald's. In place of the ancient rood screen of larger churches, the congregation now saw the symbol of the crown, flanked by the pulpit, and positioned between them and the sanctuary, wherein lay religious truth and spiritual salvation. This rather secular view of the organisation of life is, perhaps, softened by the continuity which springs from the trinity of Norman lights at the east end of the church.

Like most churches, Bonnington underwent restoration and repair in the 1800s and 1900s - the north porch, for example, was repaired with brick and plaster in 1937 - but its population declined and in 1878 it was united with the living of Bilsington, another church with a privately owned advowson. The uniting of these two livings provides a good example of the traditional solution to combining privately-owned advowsons: as late as 1963, the owners of Bilsington still held one turn at nominating the incumbent, while owners of Bonnington (a full rectory to Bilsington's vicarage) owned two turns of nomination.

ST. EANSWITH
BRENZETT

Brenzett

Brenzett, clearly, has always been a stopping-point and crossroads on the Rhee Wall, the dividing line between the Romney and Walland Marshes. To a greater extent than many churches, it exhibits very clearly the circumstances of its ownership and importance in the parish throughout the ages.

The original church may have been founded by the Saxons sometime after the death in 640 of St. Eanswith, as the dedication is an oddity: this is the only church in England dedicated solely to the founder of Folkestone Abbey. (No record of the church exists prior to the late 1100s, however, and it is possible that the church took its dedication from the moving of the Saint's remains in 1140 to Folkestone church.)

Whether it was a rebuilt Saxon church or a new building, the original Norman church of the 1100s was of standard design, consisting of the existing chancel and the eastern two bays of the nave. The original base of the chancel arch (altered at its upper levels; a common change) has some of the only visible Norman remains in the church.

The church was extended twice over the next 150 years: firstly in the early 1200s, with the addition of the narrow north aisle and the north chapel, and then in the early 1300s by the western extension of the nave to its present length. The distinctive oak-shingled spire and the south porch were added in the 1400s. These changes had a strong impact on the look of the church, altering it from a typical, rectangular Norman box-shape to a long, low and extensive-looking building. The enlargement of the church perhaps reflects the increasing importance of Brenzett in the 1300s - it was the rallying place for the marsh's contribution to the Peasant's Revolt in 1381 - as well as changing ownership of the church.

In the early 1400s, the ownership of Brenzett church was taken from the Abbey of Guynes, in Flanders, and resettled by John Kempe, the Archbishop of York, upon the College of Wye. This connection survived the Dissolution, albeit in an altered form, as grants of the advowson in both the 1500s and 1600s included provision for paying stipends to the College. Nor were these minor obligations: the first owner after the Dissolution, Walter Bucler, forfeited his ownership within a few years for not complying with the maintenance of the College's schoolmaster and curates.

A fair number of bequests are recorded, dating in particular to the 1400s and 1500s. Prior to the Reformation, such votary bequests - especially for the maintenance of candles to light saints' icons or statues - were one of the most frequent forms of ensuring that one's soul was prayed for after death. These were not large bequests, such as those left for memorial chapels, windows, or even tablets. They were, rather, private offerings which represented something of a private contract between the legatee and his god: they were certainly neither grand enough nor obvious enough to act as impressive monuments to mortal achievements.

The pre-Reformation church, with numerous statues and icons lit by candles, was of course entirely changed in the course of church history in the 1500s and 1600s. The most immediate changes, brought about by both liturgical and social forces, were surely the removal of the mediaeval chancel screen and rood beam; the "posting", by royal decree, of the royal arms after the Restoration of 1660; the introduction of box pews; and the increased importance of preaching and liturgy, resulting in acoustically efficient pulpits and the creed boards of the 18th century.

Some traditional aspects of worship remained the same, of course, the most common being the honouring of important persons by burial inside the church, the erection of monuments to their memory, and various gifts to embellish the church.

The most obvious example of this is the alabaster monument in the Lady (or north) Chapel to John Fagge and his son, covering a family vault which continued in use until well into the 18th century. Dating to the 1640s, the monument has been criticised for dominating the architecture of the chapel. The whole point of church architecture in general (and chapels in particular), however, was not to create an unsullied architectural space: it was, rather, to provide a building which would enclose the worship and establish the continuity of the parish and its inhabitants - precisely what the Fagge monument does, regardless of its impact upon the "purity" of the Lady Chapel.

Less ostentatious monuments mark other aspects of parish life. These include the 1536 chancel burial of Thomas Dekyn, a vicar; the gift of a 13th-century font in 1640 by William Somner (removed in the restoration works of 1876); the centre-aisle burial of John Wentworth (d.1770), the Rector for 32 years; a memorial tablet to Thomas Fisher (1813); a memorial window to the Rev. Tatton Brockman, vicar of Rottingdean, Sussex (and presumably a relative of Brenzett's rector, R.D. Brockman, who owned his own living here); and a carved reredos given in 1911 to the memory of the vicar from 1904-07, the Rev. C.R. Aldred. All of these elements, combined with the building itself, give a physical reflection of the continuation of parish life at Brenzett over a period of some 800 years. The general "feel" of the church, however, owes much more to successive restorations of 1826, 1876 and 1902.

The first of these involved the repair of stonework in the form of the Y-tracery windows and the west door. The second, in keeping with ideas of what was correct in liturgical terms, was more drastic, involving the removal of the box pews, the dismantling of the triple-decked, 18th-century pulpit (the sounding-board of which found its way into the vestry as a table-top), the replacement of most of the windows, the addition of the deal boarding (a much-decried feature of the church), and the provision of a new font (replacing the 13th-century font which had been found at Canterbury and brought here in 1640).

The major works of 1902 involved the complete reconstruction of the spire (which was found to be 2'6" out of perpendicular), and the virtual rebuilding of the chancel. The dormer window over the north aisle is an even later alteration, dating to 1925.

The church now stands as the embodiment of Christian life in Brenzett - perhaps not an architecturally pure building but, for that very reason, an accurate reflection of the changes witnessed by the church over some 800 years.

ST. AUGUSTINE
BROOKLAND

Brookland has many characteristics typical of Romney Marsh churches: it is suprisingly large for a village church; it is historically rich, housing the country's most important 13th-century lead font; and it is idiosyncratic, with alarmingly leaning interior walls and an enormous detached belfry topped by a weather-vane of 1797 showing a winged dragon with a forked tongue - a trenchant comment on the fickleness of marsh weather.

It is now generally held that the parish of Brookland was reclaimed about the time that the Rhee channel was formed - that is, sometime around the late 1100s. The core of the existing church seems to date to the middle of the 1200s, which would be consistent which this dating. The belfry was always detached: some of the timber appears to date to about 1260 (contemporary with the present church), although most of the structure dates to a rebuilding and recasing of c. 1450.

The church has always suffered from subsidence - the leaning of the arcades to the aisles is, along with the belfry and the lead font, one of the most memorable aspects of the church - and it may have been this recurring problem which led to the rebuilding of the 1200s, and to the addition of north and south aisles within about 100 years of this date. These later works could have dated to the time, c.1360, that the Abbey appropriated the rectorial income and established a perpetual vicarage - indeed, it seems reasonable to wonder if the income was appropriated precisely because of the cost incurred in shoring up a relatively new building by adding so much fabric.

The church saw a good deal of regular improvement - possibly a factor of its ownership before the Dissolution by the Abbey, which was continued afterwards by its being regranted to the Dean and Chapter of Canterbury Cathedral. The existing timber porch was added in the 1300s; the belfry appears to have been rebuilt in the middle 1400s; the window at the east end was replaced in the 1500s (at the same time that the existing timber roof was built); and in the next century the sanctuary was rearranged in accordance with Archibishop Laud's orders - the altar table being enclosed on three sides to prevent desecration, an arrangement still found at Fairfield church. (The 17th-century altar rails and gate were later re-sited at the entrance to the east-end chapel of the south aisle.) In 1685, the church bells were recast and expanded to provide the existing peal of five bells.

The regular rhythm of parish life continued throughout this long period, with numerous bequests to light candles in perpetuity and the placing of memorials and tombs (including one in a now-demolished Lady Chapel, probably at the east end of the north aisle, and the 1615 altar tomb of John Plomer, three times mayor of Romney, in the east chapel of the south aisle). The church thus gradually accreted the usual array of memorials, structural changes (such as buttresses), changes for liturgical reasons, and functional alterations. (Examples of the latter include the partitioning of the west end of the north aisle for a few hundred years as a small schoolroom, and the closing off of the west end of the south aisle by a carved screen in the 17th century - an area known here as the "tithe pen", as it later housed the parish's set of official weights).

In short, by the early 1700s the church was probably too cluttered to serve its parishioners properly, and a fairly major restoration and refitting was called for. This was undertaken in about 1740, and included new windows in the south aisle; lead for the aisle roof; re-tiling of other roofs; new buttresses; insertion of box pews; a new royal coat of arms (dated 1739); and the addition of a musician's gallery at the west end – perhaps, as Anne Roper suggested, re-using parts of the old rood screen and choir stalls. This also seems a likely date for the 18th-century triple pulpit (later cut down to its present size).

Later in the 18th century, the fine set of scales dated 1795 (now housed in a glass case at the west end of the church) was placed in the "tithe pen" to weigh the payment of tithes - an excellent example of the interaction between the ecclesiastical and civil parishes that was so marked in former times.

Liturgical changes in the wake of the general revival of religious feeling in the 19th century meant that some of the details of this arrangement were soon unsuitable. Thus the triple pulpit - formerly used for preaching at the top, lesson-reading in the centre, and a clerk's desk at the base - was cut down in size in 1870 (the sounding board, as at Brenzett, was re-used in the church as a table top); similarly, 10 years later, the musician's gallery was removed from the west end of the nave.

In keeping with late Victorian fashion, more comprehensive restoration was begun in the chancel, with the old floor tiles being replaced and the Laudian altar rails being removed to their present location. It proceeded no further, however, and early 20th-century work was much less drastic. In 1926, the floor tiles were

Brookland

relaid, while in 1936 the belfry's black tarred shingles were replaced with cedar wood shingles.

Damage during World War II was severe, and it was not until the mid-1950s that proper repairs began. This involved repair rather than restoration, but nonetheless major works were demanded. The east wall of the south aisle, along with its Perpendicular window, was taken down and rebuilt, all of the chancel windows were reglazed in clear glass, and a war memorial clock was erected in the turret stairs beside the north porch. This work continued in a more drastic form throughout the 1960s, with hidden reinforcement of the structure, much re-roofing - including replacement of a cast-lead roof on the north aisle with copper - and replacement of the nave aisle floor. This last task demanded shifting of the worm-ridden 18th-century box pews, a move which led to their complete disintegration.

While now representing a substantially repaired building - it could not be otherwise, given subsidence and war damage - Brookland church undoubtedly rewards examination. Its particular historic elements - the spectacular font, and the good peal of 17th-century bells - are perhaps of specialised interest, but the building in general is particularly intriguing as a record of change over time, and the attitude of different ages to the vexed question of repair and restoration.

ALL SAINTS
BURMARSH

Burmarsh is one of the marsh's most ancient villages and churches, tucked away at the eastern extremity of the marsh. The manor, to which the advowson was appended, was given as early as 848 to St. Augustine's Abbey; after the Dissolution, the Crown granted away the manor but kept the rights of patronage itself, and Burmarsh then remained under Crown patronage for over 300 years.

The plan of the church is that of a typical Norman church built within a century of the Conquest, with a single and tiny aisleless nave - it measures just 31 by 19 feet, the "footprint" of a Victorian terraced house - leading to an equally simple chancel. The chancel would have been lit by small round-headed windows to the east, along with similar windows to the north and south. Of these, the south window was blocked, and the east window replaced in the 1300s; the north light remains as the only surviving window from the original church of the mid-1100s.

Some sort of tower was in existence by about 1200, as evidenced by the plain Early English arch to the nave, but this was rebuilt in the 1300s. This rebuilding, along with the massive buttresses to the tower and the south side of the nave, underline Burmarsh's greatest problem: the peat foundations here were constantly shrinking, and much remedial work was called for. It may also account for the odd relationship between the height of the chancel and that of the nave. Chancel roofs are usually lower than those of naves not, as here, considerably higher (a fact which the battlements to the side walls fail to hide). It has been surmised that an early collapse of the nave and chancel arch might account for the rebuilding of the nave at its lower level, the loss of the chancel arch - a notable missing feature - and the lack of side aisles. This seems reasonable as regards the nave and chancel arch: the configuration is exceedingly odd, and it may also account for such an early rebuilding of the tower. The lack of aisles, however, could have been less a matter of poor building conditions than of the 14th-century cost of rebuilding the nave of what was, after all, quite a new building.

Burmarsh in the 1300s was certainly not too poor to undertake major works, as witnessed by the replacement of the original Norman east window, the rebuilding of the tower, and other necessary works such as the apparent moving of the west door to the south side of the church. This door, now the church's main entrance, and the most impressive of its Norman remains, seems to be too large for its present position, with some of its height hidden from view.

The south door was not only too large for its new position: it also proved to be too large for later generations who had to replace the wooden door, and was made smaller in the 1500s by inserting a secondary doorcase. This work may date to the same time that the stone porch was added, either shortly before or shortly after the Crown took over the advowson from St. Augustine's Abbey in the 1530s. That parts of the building were in poor repair by the early 1500s cannot be doubted, as at least one bequest - of two sheep, in 1508, from William Arminand of Orgarswick - was for the repair of the two-light window in the south wall of the nave by the porch.

Little appears to have occurred in physical terms for some 200 years after the church's living came under Crown patronage in 1538, other than the usual insertion of monuments which is found in an active parish church. In the 1700s, however, extensive new work was undertaken to accommodate the new fashions of privately-owned box pews, a triple pulpit with an inlaid sounding-board, and a 3-panelled, Georgian-framed reredos for the altar. These features, the first two of which were introduced in almost all of the marsh churches

Burmarsh

during the course of the 18th century, were accompanied by new nave windows - perhaps a sign of long-term neglect of the fabric at this small village church.

George III's coat of arms on the south wall - unusually signed by the artist - probably dates to the late 1700s. This was a distinct feature of the English church after the Restoration, as a decree of 1660 required each church to display the arms as a reminder of the sovereign's supremacy over the church.

The 19th century revival of religious life saw an increase in the provision of gifts and memorials, such as those to members of the Coleman family. In 1877, however, as was the fashion at all good parishes, a major restoration was begun, stripping out the Georgian box pews, the triple-decker pulpit, and the reredos and altar rails, and refixing the wall monuments. The only remnants of earlier fittings now remaining are the 18th-century oval blackboard text on the tower screen, and two ancient benches, placed in the porch during the works of 1877-79.

It is usual to damn in uncomprising terms Victorian restorations such as this. Developments in the church during the course of the 19th century, however, had led to a strong revival and a renewed discipline in matters liturgical, and it is hardly suprising to find that fittings in a tiny parish church, seen at the time as 100-year-old relics of a more secular age, were considered completely disposable. Arguments raged, it is true, over the ruination of ancient buildings, but these tended to be concerned either with the false Gothicisation of early buildings, or with the removal of all traces of life which had accreted after the erection of the structure.

Burmarsh's restoration thus addressed the needs of the church in its day, not least by opening up new space for improvements, memorials and gifts. These included the tuning and rehanging of the bells, two of which, still in use, date to c.1375; a new reredos, given in 1897-1900 by the then-rector, the Rev. Edmund Ibbotson; and a good modern screen between the nave and the chancel (in place of the "missing" chancel arch), erected in 1923 as a memorial to two parish men who died in the first World War. In spite of the restoration of 1877-79, which removed a great deal of the church's intermediate historical fittings, the ancient Norman church - no more than just a chancel, nave and tower - still bears witness to over 800 years of the spiritual life of this small community of the marsh.

ST. PETER AND ST. PAUL
DYMCHURCH

Structurally, this church has had two configurations. The first was the Norman church, erected in c.1150 and given a tower a century later. This small building served the population of its rather poor parish until the early 19th century, at which time the existing church was created by extending and re-working the Norman building. Engravings give a good idea of the original church: a standard nave, chancel and porch of about 1150, with a tower added to the west end in the 1200s.

The placing and design of this tower was interesting, and had a great impact on the re-working of the church some 600 years later. Early engravings show that it was built within the body of the church - that is, with its outer wall flush with the west wall of the nave - and that it was supported by two enormous buttresses to either side of the west door of the church. The 19th century tower was built between the buttresses, and the old west door now forms the entrance arch from the tower to the church; the 13th-century window above (now in the gallery) was, of course, originally on the outside wall of the tower.

The advowson of the church, anciently owned by St. Augustine's abbey, was retained by the Crown after the Dissolution, but little appears to have changed at Dymchurch for hundreds of years. The reason is not difficult to find. An inventory of 1552 shows a very poor parish in comparison with other churches of the marsh - one that had no church plate, having sold its only chalice to raise some money.

What this meant in practice was that the church was not greatly altered. Its fortunes, however, seem to have picked up in the late 1600s and throughout the 1700s, at which time a number of monuments and memorials appear in the building. Examples include a tablet above the south nave recess to Captain Timothy Bedingfield (the founder of an educational charity who died in 1693), and a memorial in the chancel floor to John Fowle (a clerk to the Lords of Romney Marsh who succeeded his father in the same office and died in 1753).

This increased status of some of Dymchurch's parishioners led to some modest improvements and gifts. The chancel floor was relaid in 1717 (the date shown on one of the tiles near the vestry door); a chalice was given in 1732; and a wine flagon was given in 1780. The royal arms, required by a law of 1660 to be played in all churches, and now mounted on the west gallery, are dated 1778; they were painted by the same artist who created similar arms for Brenzett two years later.

This increased wealth and parish activity eventually made the little Norman church too small, and enlargement was undertaken in 1821. The major change at this time was the removal of the north wall of the Norman nave, and the extension of this side of the church with a new roof covering the whole of the enlarged church. The tower of the 1200s was removed, and a new tower was built between the two huge buttresses of the earlier work. (This re-use of the older structure has meant that the existing tower is centred on the line of the old nave, rather than that created by the expansion of the church to the north in 1821.) Internally, new deal pews were added, the old pews being said to have been used for wainscotting; if so, this has since been removed. In addition, the west gallery was added in the extra space created by removing the tower from the body of the church, and new windows were probably added to the chancel. This expansion of Dymchurch was quite different to later Victorian restorations, as it was a direct response to a growing population rather than a desire to up-date or "restore" the church. The "new" church of 1821 served the parish for 90 years before works were again required.

In 1910, the chancel arch and south wall were underpinned; new floor tiles were laid; the vestry was added (a feature which removed a Norman priests' door in the north wall of the chancel); and the Norman south porch was replaced. The high altar was also replaced, the original altar being repositioned to its present site south of the chancel arch.

This work presaged a great deal of improvement in the inter-war period. In 1923, a new organ was placed in the gallery; four years later a memorial window was placed in the east window (designed by F. Conrad Eden, and much admired), and angel lights were added in the chancel. Many more embellishments followed in the 1930s: the three bells were rehung in 1931; oak clergy stalls were added in 1934; the south nave window (showing the Epiphany) was placed in 1935; choir stalls were added in 1937; and the north nave window (showing the Ascension) was inserted in 1938.

War damage appears to have been restricted mainly to the 19th-century chancel windows (replaced, other than for the east window, in 1957). Post-war work of 1958 included repairs to the walls, a start to the replacement of the 19th century pews and, sadly, the replacement of the Norman timberwork to the roof of the chancel. The church now stands as a good example of a building which, through enlargement and refitting, clearly illustrates its 800 years of history as the centre of parish life.

Dymchurch

ST. MARY
EAST GULDEFORD

East Guldeford is an exception to the rest of the churches in this guide, and belies its late mediaeval rather than ancient origins by its structure of brick. The need for a church came about with the inning from the late 1400s of the Guldeford Level, part of the Playden salt marshes, by Sir Richard Guldeford. (The freehold of the surrounding lands were not granted to his descendants, however, until 1552-53.)

The church, with but few alterations, still stands as it was built in the first years of the 16th century, sometime after 1505. It is a simple rectangular box, with only a wooden rood beam marking the transition from nave to chancel (although a screen would undoubtedly have existed here when the church was first built). Decoration was provided by the painted frieze of angels at the east end, presumably supplemented prior to the removal of Catholic images.with the usual array of icons, candles, rood screen and cross.

This was a modern and a privately-owned church, and there was probably little call for substantial change while it remained with the Guldeford family. The advowson of the church, however, was leased out from at least 1610, and within 110 years the Guldefords had ended their formal connection with the church. (In 1689, the advowson was sold to Richard Cooke, and 30 years later the site of the church and the surrounding fields - thought until then to be glebe lands, but never dedicated as such - were sold to Henry Farmer.)

East Guldeford

Interestingly, this disappearance of the Guldefords from the scene marks the start of a period of revival at St. Mary's: perhaps the purchase of the site of the church was spurred by neglect of the building. In any event, 18th century embellishments and changes were soon forthcoming: a silver cup was given in 1728; a bell of 1740 was placed above the west entrance; and deal pews and a triple-decked pulpit were added in accordance with liturgical practice of the time.

In 1764 - perhaps the date of the pews and other woodwork - the roof was repaired and the present double, hipped roof with a central valley was introduced. The roof was originally supported by four timber posts which ran down the centre of the church, and this may account for the wide aisle; the posts were removed in the early 20th century, when the roof was reinforced with steel beams. This re-roofing - mentioned in a county history of 1835 - may have coincided with the addition of the large buttresses on the west and south sides of the building. Certainly, two hundred years of virtual neglect may have undermined both the roof and the walls of the church.

St. Mary did not last much longer as a separate parish, being annexed c.1790 to the living of Playden. The combined rectory and tithes were sold to Thomas Lamb in 1792, and for the next 120 years the advowson of the combined living was often owned by the incumbent himself or by his family.

The church remained as a rural outpost, lacking even a firm access path across the marshes as late as 1835. An intriguingly late set of royal arms - showing the arms of George IV, who did not ascend the throne until 1820 - contribute to the 18th-century tone of this strangely appealing embodiment of the marsh's tradition of low church architecture.

ST. THOMAS-A-BECKET
FAIRFIELD

Especially when it floods, the image of Fairfield church is surely one of the most poignant to be found on the marsh: a tiny oasis of spiritual life, stubbornly withstanding centuries of encroachment by the sea.

The dedication suggests a foundation of the late 1100s, within a few years of Becket's martyrdom in 1170. It was probably erected when this part of the Walland Marsh was inned - a new church was a standard feature of manors found at this time - but it is tempting to see it as an outpost for pilgrims going on to the saint's shrine at Canterbury. The first reference to the little church dates to 1238 when its owner, the Priory of Christ Church, appropriated the income and established a perpetual curacy.

The plan is consistent with a date of about 1200, being a simple Norman building of nave, chancel and south porch, and a tower built into the body of the church. Unlike the marsh's other Norman churches, however, Fairfield was timber-framed, and the salt and water of the marsh were always unkind to timber. It is not surprising to find that as early as 1294 the structure was in poor repair; the Priory probably had to repair the building a number of times prior to the Dissolution, when the advowson was regranted to the Dean and Chapter of Canterbury and then leased out along with the manor of Fairfield.

Presumably some time after the Dissolution, the external timberwork finally rotted away, and the Norman timber frame was cased in brick. No change was made to the plan, however, and what now exists is a timber-framed building of Norman plan, preserved in a brick shell four or five hundred years younger.

The manor and church continued to be leased out, with at least five different known lessees in the 1600s. In 1706, however, the lease was taken by Sir Henry Furnese, and then passed through marriage to the Earls of Guilford, with whom it remained for at least the rest of the century. It is to this tenure that the fine box pews, triple-decked pulpit, and Commandments Board date - a rare and unusually complete survival of 18th-century church fittings which were

Fairfield

once found in almost all of the marsh's rural churches.

It was undoubtedly Fairfield's isolation - it has never served an obvious parish population - which saved the fittings from the 19th-century fate which befell similar arrangements at other churches. In 1869, the parish was united with Brookland, yet again underlining the lack of any indigenous population in Fairfield.

By the early 1900s, the timber structure was again threatening to collapse, and in 1912-13 the church was virtually taken down and rebuilt. It now stands, isolated as it has been for almost 800 years, surrounded only by the grazing livestock of the marsh.

ST. GEORGE
IVYCHURCH

Ivychurch

There was undoubtedly an ancient building on this site - rectors are known from the 1240s, and traces of 13th-century work have been found - but the existing church of St. George dates to a complete rebuild of about 1360 - 1370. This rebuilding was so complete that the church was almost certainly given a new dedication, to England's "new" patron saint (commonly accepted as such only after the Order of the Garter was founded in 1350). Although not unknown, the re-dedication of a church is an extremely rare occurrence.

Perhaps the old church had become so ruinous that it was considered virtually vacant; if so, the new building was to suffer the same fate, for its history has been one of long periods of neglect followed by substantial renovation. The root of this recurring problem is that this very fine building was erected on a truly grand scale, quite unrelated to the size of the parish's population, and one of the largest village churches in England.

In terms of its structure, the church is still very much as it was built in the late 1300s, with three aisles of equal length, no chancel arch, clerestory windows, and a large tower complete with a beacon turret at its northeast corner

This beacon, or outlook turret, and the tower and porch embattlements, may provide a clue to the rebuilding of the church: what was later known as the Hundred Years War had begun in the 1330s, and this was a particularly fraught period of French raids. Perhaps the rebuilding - and the new dedication to England's patron saint -combined elements of religious offering, a proclamation of the righteousness of England's cause, and a reassurance of the people of the marsh that invasions would be strongly opposed.

Whatever the reason, the new church was an impressive monument, and many early features still exist. These include the west window of the north aisle; the Decorated windows of the south aisle; the altar platform, window and other details at the east end of the south aisle; and possibly the fragment of mural painting found in the northeast chapel.

Much work was undertaken in the late 1400s, although whether this was a result of damage to the fabric, pious offering, or merely fashionable upgrading is unclear. It included the replacement of the nave roof (a suprising thing if the original roof still existed), numerous new windows including the great east window and that (later blocked) in the north-east chapel, the font, a new west entrance door, and new carved wooden stalls and rood screen. (The screen was cut down, leaving just the solid panelled base, after its removal was ordered for liturgical reasons in the late 1500s.) These late Perpendicular works were accompanied by bequests such as the altar table in the northeast chapel, given by Richard Rolff in 1463.

There is little evidence of further work over the next 200 years, other than the post-Reformation removal of icons, rood screens and crosses. In the 1600s, however, some new fittings were placed, including the altar rails, four of the peal of five bells (in 1624), and the screen to the tower arch, dated 1686. These improvements continued into the 18th-century, with re-roofing of the south aisle (1703), recasting of one of the bells (1724), re-roofing of the north aisle (1728), and the fitting of box pews. The framed copy of the Thanksgiving Prayer of 1746, ordered to be read in every church, and the royal arms of 1775 (still in their original frame, although repainted in 1969) are strong reminders of the secular nature of the 18th century church.

After this period of 18th-century activity, an even more serious period of neglect began. Ivychurch was even known for housing smugglers, with vaults below the north aisle being used for storage when the nave was either too obvious or too full. (Other means of storing goods were quite blatant, with services simply being cancelled when the building was filled with contraband.)

Not surprisingly, the neglected building decayed, and by 1900 it was virtually in ruins. When a new rector was appointed in 1903, he found a formidable task: the roof had gaping holes; almost all the windows were broken; the box pews were broken and their floors were rotten; the building was infested with vermin; the churchyard was completely overgrown; and the rectory was uninhabitable.

There followed seven years of renovation, considered at the time as something of a miracle. During this restoration the box pews were removed and used to close off the north aisle for a Sunday School. (The pews were not replaced, a feature which, combined with the absence of a chancel arch, gives even more of the feel of a cathedral.) Minor improvements included the cleaning of white paint from the 17th-century tower screen and the removal in 1919 of a lead spire on top of the beacon turret of the tower.

Unfortunately, the cycle of repair and decay soon began again – a depressingly familiar problem with oversized village churches. Much work was done in the late 1960s, with the repair of walls, roofs, timberwork and windows (including complete replacement of the two westernmost windows of the south aisle), but by the 1980s the north aisle was once again totally unusable and decaying.

St. George's burden has always been that it was conceived and realised on too grand a scale for its parish to support, leading to long periods of neglect and decay. Its glory, however, lies in the breadth of vision of its builders, and this feeling of great optimism, strong religious fervour, and superb sense of religious space still reaches out across 600 years of history.

ALL SAINTS
LYDD

All Saints has long enjoyed colloquial status as "Cathedral of the Marsh", a title which undoubtedly reflects the great size of the building, but which could equally refer to the church's status as one of the earliest of all the churches of the marsh.

All Saints seems to have been founded by the 700s - a century when the Saxon town was extremely important - although the first church may have been built when the town was given to the Archbishop of Canterbury by Offa in 775. It is thought that the original building was a small apsidal basilica - i.e., a hall with two aisles - sited at the west end of the existing north aisle, as remnants of a Saxon building exist in the external walls here.

Whatever the date of these Saxon remains, the Normans built a new chancel and nave to the east of the old church, approximately in the centre of the building we now see. This may have reflected a simple desire by the conquerors to establish their religious presence at this important Saxon site; alternatively, the old building may have suffered during the successive invasions of the late Saxon period, and may not have been fit to rebuild.

This small early Norman building was expanded greatly in the middle of the 1200s, with the addition of the east end and side aisles to within three bays of the existing west end of the church. This was the century in which most churches saw the addition of aisles and other elaborations, but the scale of the work at Lydd marks the continuing importance of the town. Unfortunately, Lydd's dependency upon the sea was underlined within decades of the building of this new, expanded church: the great storms of the 1200s shifted the course of the river and sealed Lydd's fate forever.

In retrospect, the storms of the late 1200s were unquestionably the turning point for Lydd. Nonetheless, the decline took centuries, as did the realisation that Lydd's days as a centre of power on the marsh were numbered. In the meantime, practical assistance was given: three years after the storm, Lydd was made a corporate member of the Cinque Ports under New Romney, and even the appropriation in 1321 of the rectory by Tintern Abbey (the owners of the church) may mark an administrative mechanism for improving the church rather than merely a means of improving Tintern's income. As befitted its status, the church also continued to be embellished and expanded: the great tomb identified as that of Sir Walter de Meryl was added in the 1300s; in the 1400s, the nave was extended to the west by three bays and the east windows were replaced; a monumental brass - now the earliest in the church - marked the burial in 1429 of John Thomas; and the tower was added in the mid 1440s under no less a person than the senior mason at Canterbury, Thomas Stanley.

The mid 1400s were years of great piety in England, as well as a time of peace after the century-long war with France which so seriously undermined the fabric and the society of the marsh. It is perhaps this century of neglect and the new era of peace which on the one hand made such extensive work necessary, and on the other attracted the funds needed to carry out the work. Certainly a number of bequests for the reparation of the roof were made in the period from 1444-1484, and it was presumably these which were used to raise the fine king-post roof.

The end of this period of building came with the raising of the tower to its present height in the early 1500s, and All Saints then lived a fairly quiet life for about 350 years. It remained, however, as perhaps the single most important church of the marsh, a fact which accounts for its continued embellishment with fine tombs and beautiful fittings. The tomb of Clement Stuppenye, dated 1608, doubled as the place for electing the Bailiff and Jurats of Lydd; equally impressive was the fine bust on the north wall of Thomas Godfrey, who died in 1623. Embellishments of the next century included the font and two chandeliers dated 1753 and 1786, which would have complimented the insertion of Georgian box pews and the other liturgical necessities of the 18th century.

As a town, however, Lydd had become something, quite literally, of a backwater, and things did not begin to change until the late 1870s and early 1880s. In 1879, the military camp was established; three years later, the arrival of the railway made renovation essential and in 1887, among other works, the box pews were removed, the floor was renewed, and gas lighting and coal heating were provided.

This was drastic work, but one statistic speaks volumes: by replacing the box pews with new, forward-facing pews, the seating capacity of the church was increased from 458 to 1,200. The problems faced by the resurgent church of the 19th century, and the reason why so many churches removed fittings designed uniquely for 18th-Century conditions of worship, are surely here starkly outlined: no matter how fine the craftsmanship of Georgian church-fitters, the Victorian church often had to house three times the number of communicants, and also had to provide a setting for more formal patterns of worship than had been the case a century earlier.

Little work would have been necessary after this major renovation of the late 1880s if it were not for the bombing of the east end by a direct hit on 15 October, 1940. This completely destroyed the chancel, along with two of the three east windows of the 1400s. The renovation of the building - largely completed by 1953, although the chancel was finished five years later - is a remarkable and heartening continuation of 1,200 years of devotion lavished on the church by the people of Lydd.

Lydd

ST. PETER AND ST. PAUL
NEWCHURCH

In spite of its name, Newchurch appears to have existed by the middle 900s, as it gave its name to one of the Hundreds which were introduced to Saxon local government about that time. Curiously, however, it contains no physical evidence of late Saxon or early Norman building, as the existing church appears to date to the early 1200s; the church which now exists is thus something of a "new" Newchurch.

At the end of the century (in 1297), Newchurch was given a vicarage in place of its original rectorship. Curiously, however, the rectorial income was not appropriated by the patron, the Archbishop: the living was kept as a separate patronage appointment, but was made sine cure.

Newchurch

This may have been an organisational move to enable the parish to improve its accommodation; in any event, the church was enlarged and considerably embellished in the 1300s. Features which date from this period are the aisles, arcades and east chapels, the north porch, and the carved vestments chest which is now used as the altar of the northeast chapel.

Newchurch continued to improve its church in the following century – perhaps, once again, being assisted by the re-endowment of the perpetual vicarage in 1404. One of the first additions was the tower. This was begun in the early years of the century, when it started to tilt quite alarmingly – as it still does. It was then buttressed and left to find its own settled level, and was not finished until the late 1470s. In the interim, the church was given numerous bequests by its parishioners, an indication of a thriving community. It was also supplied with a new rood screen, part of which is now used for screens to the two east-end chapels.

The most interesting embellishment of the late 1400s is undoubtedly the font, as it includes Yorkist, Lancastrian and Tudor roses along with crossed keys and swords as Symbols of the parish's two patron saints. Almost certainly this dates to the period of peace after Henry VII accession in 1485 which finally ended the Wars of the Roses, offering a pleasing connection between the history of the parish and that of the nation.

Renovation in the 1500s included a new roof with good carved Tudor bosses, as well as repairs to the chancel (reported in 1511 as being in disrepair). The parish then seems to have gone into a something of a slow decline: in spite of bequests such as an extremely valuable silver chalice of 1568, the population sank by the 1630s to just 8 adults.

Newchurch

Oddly enough, revival was at hand, marked by the provision of a new peal of five bells in 1637, and a fine Jacobean pulpit with its sounding board – still complete, and predating the fashion for box pews and triple-decked pulpits. The parish seems to have remained at this intermediate level for another 200 years, as additions such as the prayer and commandment boards (now by the vestry at the west end of the south aisle) mark liturgical and practical changes rather than increasing local fortunes. By the mid 1840s, however, the forces of change within the church could not be ignored, and a typical Victorian restoration was begun. This included the insertion of a new east window, overhaul of the bells and, presumably, removal of box pews.

20th-Century restorations have included major work in 1909-15 (the period to which the high altar cross dates), and substantial roofing, stonework and belfry repairs in the late 1960s. The church was probably always a bit large for its congregation - although now not as much so as in the 1600s - but it still contains much evidence of the changing fortunes of Newchurch over time.

ST. NICHOLAS
NEW ROMNEY

It could be said that the church of St. Nicholas has seen more changes than any other on the marsh. Its structure was expanded twice by the middle of the 14th century; its community changed even more, with the river disappearing in the 1200s and the land level rising from continued silting witnessed by the level of the west door); and four other mediaeval parish churches were completely lost to history. In a sense, St. Nicholas became New Romney's parish church by default.

The first Norman church, erected about 1100, extended five bays east of the tower and originally faced a small chancel. In the early 1200s, the lower three stages of the tower were added (leaving the exterior decoration of the church's west wall exposed below the tower platform), and the superb Norman west door was moved to the front of the tower. Within about a hundred years of these changes, the top two stages of the tower were added, aisles were built out to surround the tower's base, and the east end was completely rebuilt as we see it now: three parallel chapels, with the aisle roofs raised to above clerestory height. (Almost contemporary with these improvements is the ancient floor brass of William Holynoke, near the organ, dating to 1375.)

Whether or not these improvements were related to the giving of the church in 1264 to the priory of Potigny in France is unclear. Whatever their involvement in the early 14th century, however, the "alien masters" eventually appropriated the church's income (in 1384) and, perhaps unwisely, did not endow a vicarage for another 18 years. (If this was finally done to appease the English king, it didn't work: alien priories were suppressed in 1414, and the advowson of New Romney was given in 1438 to All Souls' College, Oxford.)

Not much change has since occurred to St. Nicholas's structure, and indeed the history of the church seems to have been relatively quiet until the 1600s.

New Romney

This probably had much to do with the extreme decline in New Romney's fortunes, as the other four mediaeval parish churches fell out of use in the first 30 years of the 16th century. The only notable relic from this time appears to be the brass of 1510 in the northeast (or Lady) chapel to Thomas Lambard.

In the 17th century, however, St. Nicholas again seems to have become quite a thriving parish - perhaps the disappearance of any competition from other town parishes had a silver lining after all - and a number of fine monuments made their appearance. Of particular note are the altar tomb and brass of the northeast chapel (1616, to Thomas Smyth); a similar altar tomb in the southeast chapel (erected in 1622 as a meeting-place for civil elections, in memory of Richard Stuppenye); a fine marble tomb of 1653 for Thomas Tookey, again in the northeast chapel; an oak screen of 1662 for the tower entrance; and a number of family tombs dating to between 1650 and 1750.

St. Nicholas was clearly wealthy at this time, and it is particularly pleasing to find embellishments other than tombs dating to the same period. Queen Anne's royal arms, for example (1707, in the southeast chapel) are nicely complemented by the church's Georgian chandelier of 1745.

St. Nicholas remained untouched until the 1880s, when a particularly heavy handed "restoration" was begun. This became something of a cause celebre, leading to an early S.P.A.B. protest and the virtual end of rebuilding churches in the guise of restoring them.

This intervention on behalf of historical continuity was an admirable movement; as has been stressed throughout this book, however, regardless of the severity of the works one must look at the motives behind Victorian changes in the same light as one would discuss, say, post-Reformation cleansing of graven images, or the insertion of Royal arms after the Restoration, or the use of secularised box-pews by the Georgians. It is only by placing a church and its development within its particular historical and religious setting that one can reach a deeper understanding of the life of parish churches such as St. Nicholas - a church which still speaks of the continuity of worship in New Romney, in spite of that town's diminished status, and partly because of the ever-changing demands of architectual and liturgical fashion.

New Romney

ST. CLEMENT
OLD ROMNEY

Like many of the marsh churches, St. Clement's seems perfectly suited to its setting and yet has peculiarities which set it apart from any other church. The church exhibits remarkably constant embellishment and development - a fact which suggests that the parish's prosperity continued in spite of the decline in its status marked by the prefix "Old" - and although many parishes can boast such continuity, what makes St. Clement's particularly interesting is the fact that many of the embellishments still exist, giving us a building which speaks volumes of its development over the centuries.

The nave and chancel, like those of most of the marsh's churches, was erected by the Normans in the 1100s; aisles and side chapels were added in the 1200s, reflecting either increasing wealth of the parishioners or changes in the ownership of the advowson. (This was given in 1140 to Arrouaise Abbey, but passed within a century to the family of de Romenal.)

The 1300s saw more additions, such as the replacement of the east windows to the chancel and south chapel, a new north porch, and the insertion of a tower in the westernmost bay of the south aisle. This last insertion, with the tower flush with the west wall of the nave, gives the church a distinct configuration which is quite different to that of a standard English church with a centralised west tower. What is rather suprising, given all this work, is that the usual replacement or opening-up of the chancel arch was not carried out: the round-headed arch which exists today is a truly rare Norman survival.

These improvements of the 14th century were followed in the 1400s by screens across the chancel, and between the chancel and its flanking chapels. These were, of course to be removed in accordance with the general order of 1569, but other remains still bear witness to the continued vitality of the parish as well as to the wider changes which affected the church over the next 300 years. The list of such changes at St. Clement's is notably long and remarkably unbroken: it includes a brass of c.1510 to John and Margaret Ips; a 1526 memorial to their son, another John Ips; an early Jacobean pulpit - perhaps the first to be introduced after the order of 1603 that all churches were to have a pulpit; a new bell of 1634; a communion cup and paten of 1692; new altar rails, tripledeck pulpit, box pews and west-end minstrel's gallery in the early 1700s; the 1738 burial in the chancel of John Deffray, a French exile who was the rector for almost 50 years; the panelling in wood of the chancel arch and screen walls facing the nave (a change which probably dated to the late 1780s, but which was removed in 1930); and the supplying of a new set of royal arms in 1800.

The continuity represented by these details - even given that the Georgian fittings have been altered or removed - is truly astounding, and suggests that the parish was always a healthy one. Additionally, St. Clement's seems to have slept quietly through the 19th century, with no great demands being made to update the building; the church thus did not suffered the worst excesses of Victorian restoration. The only changes which are immediately apparent were the insertion in 1885 of stained glass in the north chapel (by T.H. Oyler); the rebuilding of the north porch; and the blocking of the arch from the nave to the tower in 1886. Nonetheless, St. Clement's turn at modernisation was to come, in the form of extensive repairs and alterations in 1930.

The late date of this restoration, and the writing of the church's history within the living memory of those who undertook the work, has meant that judgement has been less severe than would have been the case if the works had been done, say, in the 1880s. This reflects more a harsh view of the Victorians than it does a soft judgement of their 20th-century equivalents, as the ruthlessness of the "restoration" was in truth every bit as pronounced as would have been the case 50 years earlier.

Some of the work was unquestionably beneficial: the south chapel, which was filled with rubbish, was cleared out; the original altar stone was discovered and placed in the north chapel; and the wooden gates between the south chapel and the chancel, found among the rubbish, were replaced. In addition, however, the triple-decked pulpit was cut down to form a pulpit and reading desk; the high box pews were cut down to their present height; 18th-century panelling between the chancel and the chapels, along with that to the chancel arch and screen wall was stripped off to expose the Norman chancel arch; the sanctuary was extended by moving the early 18th-century rails forward by two feet; and a plaster ceiling to the chancel was removed to expose the roof – all changes, to be fair, which would have been typical of any church restoration of the 1800s.

The restored church suffered from neglect during the war, and in 1959 the sanctuary walls were strengthened, the roofs of the nave and south aisle were repaired and restored; and the tower, which had split from top to bottom and was quickly becoming unstable, was pinned back together. Ironically, the radical changes of 1930 did not affect the choice of the church shortly after this as a location for the early 1960s movie, "Dr. Syn", for which project Rank films further restored the church. Presumably, the survival of the minstrel's gallery (the steps of which were replaced as part of the restoration) and the cut-down box pews provided sufficient authenticity, even given the loss of the tripledecked pulpit and 18th-century chancel panelling. The interest and support of the Rank organisation in the early 1960s was matched by further parochial work, with the royal arms being restored in 1965 and a new west door of 1967.

The interior of St. Clement's, although heavily restored and repaired, embodies a continuous record of over 800 years of worship on the marsh; its exterior, with Romney Marsh sheep grazing in the churchyard, presents an even more deepseated sense of the continuity of English worship, and of the men and women who called this their parish church.

Old Romney

ST. MARY MAGDALENE
RUCKINGE

St. Mary Magdalene, like the nearby churches of Bilsington and Bonnington, is an ancient church built on the "shore" of the marsh. The date of its foundation is uncertain, but was undoubtedly early: the manor of Ruckinge was granted by Offa in 791 to Christ Church, Canterbury, and it is likely that the priory built some sort of local church soon afterwards.

At the time of the Conquest, the manor and church were given to William's half-brother, Bishop Odo of Bayeux. Odo fell out with the Conqueror, however, and within ten years the estate was given to the Archbishop; he in turn kept the church and gave the manor back to the priory, where they both remained. Soon after this, in the 1100s, the nave and chancel were rebuilt in stone - probably replacing a simple wooden building erected by the Saxon overlords.

There have often been theories as to the impact on the marsh churches of so many estates being owned by Canterbury, with both Augustine's Abbey and the cathedral priory having extensive holdings. The impact seems less than one might expect, however, and all of the marsh churches -

Ruckinge

corporately or privately owned - seem to follow a similar pattern of development. Ruckinge thus expanded in the course of the 1200s, with some changes reflecting developing liturgies - aisles and arcades were added - and others reflecting embellishments such as the raising of the tower by an additional stage. Still other changes of the 1200s were structural or pragmatic: the filling-in with an arch of the west door may reflect a wish to down-size the doorcase (perhaps when new doors were needed), or may have been needed to stabilise the tower in the notoriously unstable conditions of the marsh. Further improvements came in the 1300s, when the chancel arch and some of the windows were replaced, but by and large the church seems to have remained unchanged for hundreds of years.

This does not mean, however, that the parish was either derelict or destitute: in the 1400s and 1500s, bequests from its parishioners were given for many improvements, from paving the floor (in 1464) to new windows (1489 and 1513), new seating (1515), and a new treble bell (1529). Later in the same century the roof was replaced - apparently following a fire, and possibly dating to severe lightning-fires known to have occurred in the area in 1559. (As can be seen, the new roof was built on a different line to that of the centre line of the chancel.)

The Dissolution had little effect in terms of the church building, as the manor and advowson were held by the Crown for just two years before being re-granted to the Dean and Chapter of Canterbury. More serious was depopulation over the next 150 years: a 96-year-old man in 1705 was able to remember at least ten additional houses in the parish in his youth, attributing the depopulation to an outbreak of small pox.

Whatever the cause of the decrease in Ruckinge's population, it seems not to have affected one of the major occupations of the parishioners in the 1600s and 1700s: this was known to be a centre for smuggling, as is suggested by the well known wooden graveboard outside the south door (said to mark the grave of two brothers who unwisely added highway robbery to the more acceptable local pastime of simple smuggling). But even - or perhaps especially - during this period, embellishment of the church was never forgotten: four bells were hung in 1721, and a fifth was added in 1740.

Not much appears to have changed at Ruckinge in the 19th century, other than the obvious altering of its setting with the construction of the Royal Military Canal, and works such as the repair of the chancel roof and the provision of a new pulpit. In the 20th century, however, two separate restorations were undertaken: in 1929, the church was whitened, and the Lady Chapel and a child's corner were furnished; in the mid-1970s, the inside was again redecorated and the memorial glass screen to the belfry was added.

Ruckinge's character is satisfyingly strange and complex. From the outside, it looks to all the world to be a compact, inwardly-focussed and rather retiring parish church; the airiness and lightness one finds inside, however, hints at a deeper life, at least historically, than is apparent at first glance - perhaps as apt a built metaphor as one is likely to find for the close-knit communities of the marsh.

ST. MARY
RYE

Rye church has by far the most complex history of any of the buildings covered by this guide. The reason is obvious: while others may be as ancient, only St. Mary's has always been at the centre of a prosperous but much-ravaged town.

Political history has had a particularly important impact on the shape of the building, right from the date of its foundation. Rye and its surroundings were part of a grant given by Cnut to the Abbey of Fecamp in 1017, and this foreign ownership lasted for 200 years. The extent of any pre-Conquest church is unknown, but within fifty years of William's victory rebuilding began with a new chancel (c.1120). This was followed some 60 years later by the nave - about the time Rye seems to have become self-governing - and aisles were added in the early 1200s. The resultant building was much more grand than most Norman parish churches, with a true cruciform shape and a chancel and nave of almost equal length.

History then intervened. Rye and Winchelsea were taken by the French in 1216 and, although recaptured, peace was not achieved until the early 1240s. This was followed in 1247 by reclamation of the manor and advowson by Henry III, as a foreign-held beachhead was obviously a serious risk in times of war.

In this context, it is perhaps significant that the north chapel is usually dated to c.1220, while the south chapel is given a date of c.1250. It seems entirely possible that the wars interrupted the building of the chapels, and one wonders if the original dedication of the south chapel (to St. Clere, a dedication later transferred to the north) has anything to do with an offering for peace and stability.

During the 1300s, the church improved with north and south porches and new windows in the aisles, but the fate of the church once again became closely tied to the reality of French invasions. Rye was sacked in 1339 and 1377, two peak raiding periods in the Hundred Years War. The second raid was particularly devastating, as the tower collapsed, taking with it much of the roof, the chancel and the crossing.

The damage was repaired in the 1400s, and the present south side of the chancel, many of the arches, the south porch, and the flying buttress to the south-east corner of the chancel all date to this rebuilding. The old south porch - hard against the south transept, and later used as the Lamb family vault - may have been made into a chantry chapel at about the same time. At the end of the century, new windows were placed in the north and south walls of the transepts.

The church then enjoyed a few decades of relative stability - something of a novelty for a building which had seen almost constant change. In the middle of the 16th century, however, change once again came to the fore. In 1547 the church's chantry of St. Nicholas (founded 1281) was disendowed, and in 1551 the advowson of the vicarage was granted to the Sackville family and the rectorial income was appropriated to the Bishop of Winchester. The only positive outcome of this period of upheaval was the provision of the church clock - still operating - which dates in its mechanism to 1560. In 1569 (an important date, when all images, crosses and rood screens were ordered removed) the two east chapels were

Rye

partitioned off and secularised and the south porch and its small room were re-ordered and the door blocked up.

In an established church, state decrees are a fact of life. The parish church must continue to accommodate the changing needs of its community, however, and in the 1600s, this manifested itself in a increased attendance to hear preachers. For centuries, priests had needed a separate licence to preach, and it was not until 1603 that churches were even required to have a pulpit. It may be this change in practice which demanded more seating, and a gallery was added to the south side of the nave in the early 1600s. (The brass of Thomas Hamon, dated 1607 and found behind the high altar, is of the same period.)

Not much was done in the way of structural work, however, and by 1701 the parish was petitioning the king to have the building repaired. This was achieved over the next two years, when the building was given a spire and an extremely imposing set of royal arms. These hang above the chancel arch; they are of solid oak, measure ten by six-and-a-half feet, and weigh 500 lbs.

St. Mary's was well-treated during the 18th century, with numerous gifts of plate, repairs to the north chapel (in 1745), a chancel candelabrum (1759), a new clock face, frame and quarter-boys (1760), a peal of eight bells (1775), and a musicians' gallery at the west end of the church (late 18th-century). The congregation increased in size as well as wealth, and in 1811 an another seating gallery was added to the north side of the nave.

Clearly the church was well set for the 19th century, and it was not until about 1860 that new works began. In 1860-63, these involved restoration of the east chapels, the insertion of a large west window, and the clearing-out of the Lamb family vault for use as a vestry. The noted memorial window to Mary Tiltman, designed by Burne-Jones, was added to the north aisle in 1867. These were relatively sensitive works. Major works in 1882, however, were less cautious and were much criticised for being over-enthusiastic: the roof was replaced, all the galleries removed, the west door was blocked up, and the clerestory was entirely rebuilt. It is fair to say that the existing "feel" of the church now dates to the two periods of restoration in the 1860s and 1880s.

20th-century improvements have included the installation of new choir stalls, screen and organ (c.1901), with the south chapel being converted to a choir vestry and organ chamber. Fine inter-war memorials include the high altar (c.1922) and the Benson memorial windows in the south transept and the great west window (1928 and 1937, respectively). War damage was largely restricted to the loss of two of the three east windows; a new east window (designed by Christopher Webb) was inserted in 1952, about the same time that a major programme of structural and roofing repairs, re-hanging of the bells, and renovation of the clock frame was carried out. The clock has since been restored again (1969), at which time the much-decayed quarter-boys were recast in fibreglass and the originals retired to the north chapel.

It is, of course, St. Mary's complex history of change and development which makes the church such an intriguing building. It was never destined to be as pretty, as pastoral or as peaceful as the village churches of the marsh; it was always destined to be as clear a record of the forces which formed it.

ST. MARY THE VIRGIN,
ST. MARY IN THE MARSH

St. Mary's well illustrates a central point of the apparent "over-churching" of the marsh. The population was never great, and the church served an entirely local congregation; the parish was at times fairly poor; and yet the church was expanded and embellished over the centuries in an admirable and sometimes even grand manner.

Like many of the marsh churches, the core of the original building was erected by the Normans in the early 1100s, and the modest design was typical of its age: a simple nave, marked by the existing space between the aisles, and a chancel about half the length of that which now exists. The tower was added later in the same century - always a difficult proposition on marshland, as attested by the huge buttresses which were added to its corners in modern times. About 1270 the building was extended to its modern ground-plan, with north and south aisles, the virtual doubling of the length of the chancel, the addition of the piscina and double sedilia, and possibly the removal of the chancel arch.

These changes were similar to those found in almost all of the marsh churches, and reflect the changing liturgy and formal requirements of the church; nonetheless, they were keyed to the nature and resources of each parish. In such a small rural church, and in the absence of major benefactors, separate north and south chapels at the ends of the aisles would have been a luxury. Additional altars were nothing of the sort, however, and in this case the ends of the two were put to the same purpose. The north aisle altar, dedicated to Our Lady, took the place of a Lady Chapel; that in the south aisle was dedicated to St. Michael. (All such chapels were generally desecrated in late Elizabethan and Puritan times, and the altar now in the north aisle was placed here when the church's existing high altar was obtained from a church in Dover.)

The parish prospered for over 200 years after these improvements, with bells being added in the late 1300s and in the 1400s, and numerous bequests for the lighting of candles and burials within the church dating to the period 1460-1525. The two brasses for which St. Mary's is best known - those of Matilda Jamys (1499) and her son, William Gregory (1502) - date to the same period, as does the rebuilding of the south porch and the renewal of many of the church's windows.

The upheavals of the Reformation hit St. Mary's fairly hard, and in early 1552 the church was vandalised and lost much of its plate and vestments. Some of this was later replaced - the existing plate includes a remarkable communion cup of 1578 - but the parish never again seems to have reached its high point of about 1500. In 1588 there were but 51 communicants listed in the parish, and by 1635 - shortly after the period to which the Jacobean font cover dates - the rectorial living was among the poorest in the district.

The parish did, of course, introduce the necessary fittings for 18th-century worship, including creed and commandment boards, a new oak pulpit (c.1710), box pews, and the statutory royal arms (those displayed were painted in 1775).

It was not until the latter part of the century, however, that major improvements could be afforded - in particular the retiling of the chancel floor, done between 1780 and 1800. Much of this work was reversed during the course of the next century, when the box pews were removed and perhaps cut down to supply lower boxes - a physical reminder of the Victorian revival of the church, and of the demands placed upon church buildings by an ever-changing liturgy.

St. Mary's also shows evidence of its 20th-century parochial life with, for example, the 1924 tablet to Edith M. Nesbit (author of "The Railway Children") complementing her grave in the churchyard. Substantial repairs have involved the rebuilding of the roof and the repair of the steeple in 1932, and the church, with its high steeple visible for miles, continues to provide a concrete reminder of the fortunes and misfortunes of almost 900 years of parochial life in the sometimes harsh landscape of the marsh.

St Mary in the Marsh

ST. DUNSTAN
SNARGATE

One would assume that Snargate, dedicated to the Saxon Archbishop St. Dunstan, was an ancient pre-Conquest church. Oddly enough, however, it is now generally felt that the church was founded about the time that the Rhee channel was cut and most of the parish was inned in the late 1100s. (It remains a possibility, however, that the church was founded somewhat earlier, as parts of the future parish were apparently the subject of land grants in the 800s.)

In any event the nave was erected in the early 1200s and Snargate, like St. Clement's at Old Romney, shows an unbroken history of building and pious embellishments. It was not long after the nave was built that building works began: within about fifty years aisles were added (of slightly different lengths, suggesting either simple rural workmanship or some delay between building the two), and c.1275 a bell was provided - the latter one of the two oldest inscribed bells in Kent. This activity continued relatively unbroken for another two hundred years, with the east end being rebuilt in the 1300s as three parallel chapels. The east windows still date to this period, as does the roof of the north aisle with its carved bosses and the altar tomb of c.1360 in the north chancel arcade.

One wonders if this tomb, long stripped of its brass inscriptions and of an unknown parishioner, marks the grave of the benefactor who funded any of these extensive building works. In any event, it was not the end of improvements. The tower was added c.1400, followed by new windows in the north and south aisles and numerous bequests for improvements such as floor paving (1485), repair of the nave (1510), and the notable terracotta coloured painting of a ship (found in 1971 under whitewash, and apparently dating to the early 1500s).

The parish continued to embellish its church after the Reformation, although in accordance with the new thought this no longer took the form of mediaeval votary bequests for the lighting of candles. In about 1570 - the date when rood screens and other images were ordered removed from churches - the north and south chapels were closed off and made into rooms accessible only from the outside. (Some two centuries later, these were found to be extremely useful spaces for the storage of smuggled goods.) Again in accordance with the general changes in the form of worship, a Jacobean altar table and sanctuary rails were provided in the 1600s, as was a new bell frame (c.1650), a bell (of 1673), and a fine Late Stuart confirmation chair (c.1685). The early 1700s saw the addition of the red brick south porch, but Snargate's parishioners appear to have been increasingly concerned with the lucrative Romney Marsh side-line of smuggling. In 1743, a large amount of tobacco was seized from the belfry and vestry, and in the late 1700s the north chapel "room" was known to be used for similar storage.

It may seem ironic to modern minds that while the building was being used for illegal purposes the parishioners continued to repair and embellish their church; but it would be unwise to simplify the complex relation between civil life and religious worship in the 18th century. Suffice to point out that the usual re-equipping of the church with box pews and a triple-decked pulpit was

Snargate

carried out; the roof was repaired in the late 1770s (the tower being releaded in 1775, and other work dating to 1780), and silver plate was given in 1779 and 1791.

The practice of absentee rectors who held Snargate along with other livings added to the advantage of using the church for smuggling, and even after the regulations of 1808 required rectors to live in their parishes, the subsidiary nature of the living of Snargate meant that permission was often granted for the rector to live elsewhere. This was the case, for example, with Snargate's best-known rector - the author Richard Barham, who held the living from 1817 to 1829 along with his resident curacy of Warehorne. The great religious revival of the 19th century eventually reached Snargate, however: in 1864 the east-end chapels were reopened, and in 1871 a new rector oversaw major works. The triple-decked pulpit was cut down; the bow pews were removed and replaced; the chancel and nave floors were retiled; and a manual organ was installed.

Works to churches often seem to occur in 100-year cycles, and at Snargate a programme of works was undertaken from the late 1950s. This included the removal of lead and the tiling of the south aisle roof (1957), the gift of electric light and heat (1958), the renewal of the first-stage floor of the tower (1960), dismantling, re-fitting and re-hanging of the bells (1971), and roofing and other repairs - including the discovery and restoration of the "ship" wall painting of c.1500.

Throughout its varied life, St. Dunstan's has overseen the temporal life of its parishioners, both admirable and questionable, and has housed their pious beliefs and hopes. Each of almost 40 generations has left its mark, and the building now embodies 800 years of the human failings and noble attributes of its people.

ST. AUGUSTINE
SNAVE

The manor of Snave was established by the late 1190s, probably being one of the many new manors which were developed along with the formation of the Rhee channel in that century. The manor of Snavewick, however, to which the advowson of Snave was appendent, was much older, having been given to Augustine's Abbey as early as 848. In the early 1200s, the owner of the newer manor unsuccessfully challenged the Abbey over ownership of the church's advowson, but it is unfortunately not clear if the disputed church was a new one, or one which had existed for some time.

Whatever the case, the existing church of St. Augustine dates to the great period of stone church-building of the 1200s, a fashion which presented so many problems when dealing with the unstable foundations of the marsh: here, as elsewhere, it led to the constant addition of buttresses in a frantic attempt to keep the building from toppling over.

The church was much rebuilt in the early 1300s, including the tower and most of the west end details. It has also been surmised that the nave may have been rebuilt since the early days, as it does not align with the chancel and north chapel; perhaps this provides further evidence of an early problem with the building's foundations.

Snave

The substantial nature of churches such as Snave, where no obvious population has ever required so large a building, often leads to some confusion. The main point to be made, however, is that the size and grandeur of mediaeval churches was not a function of the needs of its parishioners, but rather of the wealth of the parish and/or the owners of the advowson. Thus the Abbey, when granted Snavewick in 848, would have supplied a standard church regardless of whether there was to be one family or ten. Similarly, when churches were being founded or rebuilt in the 1200s and 1300s, the building would have been expanded in line with the piety of its owners and the wealth of the estate, rather than purely as a reference to the size of the congregation.

That Snave has always had only a handful of parishioners is clear from the lack of embellishments in the church: the only notable additions were a bell, dating to c.1380, and a communion cup of 1554. This is not to imply that the population has always as low as we know it to have been since the registers began in the 1650s; nonetheless, it is clear from the most cursory examination of parish churches that the continuity of embellishments is probably the most reliable indicator of parochial activity and prosperity.

Snave – a full parish church – was thus never neglected to the point of desolation, but seems to have lived a quiet existence over the centuries with the only additions being those demanded by changing patterns of worship and civil life. An altar table – now in the tower-space – was added in the 1600s in compliance with the orders of the mid-1500s to destroy all stone altars; a pewter almsdish and silver plate were given in about 1700, and the requisite royal arms were posted in 1735. In 1783 the roof was re-leaded – perhaps the date of the tower turret and weathervane – and in 1795 two bells were added and the bell frame was rebuilt.

Like many parishes, Snave saw a temporary revival in the 19th century; it had doubtless become run-down, and was duly renovated in 1873, the date of most of the furnishings. (The pulpit/reading desk, however, which re-used panels of the 1400s – probably part of the rood screen – dates to 1858.) The 1873 works included retiling and raising the chancel floor; the existing font, altar and pews; the rebuilding of the chancel arch; the replacement of the east window (along with much window glass); and the insertion of a stove in the north chapel for its use as a school-room.

Some further work was undertaken immediately after the first world war, but this unusual flurry of activity at Snave was short-lived. By the late 1970s the church had become a financial burden to the united parishes of Snargate, Snave and Brenzett, and consideration was given to deconsecration for secular use – a fate which was avoided by the intervention of the Romney Marsh Historic Churches Fund. In 1983, the building was declared redundant but kept as a consecrated symbol of at least 800 years of worship in this corner of the marsh.

CHRONOLOGY

The following chronology may seem arbitary, as it is not subdivided in any manner by theme (churches, liturgy, social/political history, etc.). This insistence upon a strict chronological order is intentional, as it is meant to underline the wider social context within which churches developed and changed,

Any such chronology - particularly for the Reformation - is bound to be simplistic and to leave many questions unaddressed. Nonetheless, it is felt that a simple date-list is useful as a checklist, as well as highlighting potential links between various contemporary events.

TO 1290: EARLIEST TIMES TO THE END OF FEUDALISM

400-500	Anglo-Saxon settlement: founding of kingdoms and first establishment of manors.
597-670	Missionary phase of re-established Christian church in England. Founding of minsters and conversion of Anglo-Saxons.
668-690	Episcopacy of Theodore. Reorganisation of church, with dioceses based on Anglo-Saxon kingdoms.
From 775	Inning of Denge Marsh.
787	First Danish raids.
791	Ruckinge manor given to Canterbury.
800-1000	Main period - particularly during the 900s - for the founding of parishes in England.
848	Burmarsh and Snavewick manors given to Canterbury.
940-960	Tithes made obligatory under laws of Edmund and Edgar.
980-1035	Many new feudal holdings created by Ethelred and Cnut, and subsequent establishment of new parishes.
1042-1066	Reign of Edward the Confessor. Many manorial rights given by king and nobles to monasteries and cathedrals.
1066-1250	Norman conquest, followed by the establishment of many new manors and parishes under William and his successors.

1076	Decree by Archbishop Lanfranc that altars be of stone.
1086	Domesday. Many of the marsh churches existed by this date (although obvious exceptions such as Fairfield, Ivychurch and East Guldeford date to later centuries).
c.1100	Decree that altars be embellished with five crosses. It was this ancient use of a "sacrifical" stone altar - similar to those found in the Old Testament - which became the subject of much controversy in the post-Reformation period.
1150-1250	Construction of Rhee channel, and inning of Walland Marsh.
c. 1190	Probable date for founding of Fairfield.
1200s	French wars, including loss of Normandy (1204).
1215	Magna Carta, underlining power of landed barons.
1250-1287	Major storms, permanently shifting mouth of Rother and destroying Winchelsea.
1253	Founding of Bilsington Priory.
1262-1268	Baron's war. Although the royal party ultimately triumphed, the potential weakness of the crown against other landed interests became exceedingly clear.
1272	Accession of Edward I.
1278	Formalising of confederation of Cinque Ports.
1279	Statute of Mortmain, forbidding further acquisition of landed property by the church without royal assent.
1289	Statute of Quia Emptores, prohibiting sub-infeudination of Crown and baronial manors.
1290	Banishment of the Jews from England.

1290 -1534 MATURE MEDIAEVAL SOCIETY

1300s-1400s	Extensive establishment of chantries by nobles.
1337	Start of Hundred Years' War.
1343	Exclusion of aliens from ecclesiastical benefices.

1348-49	First occurrence of Black Death.
1351-1393	Statutes passed to check papal claims for nominating priests, and to protect rights claimed by the Crown from papal encroachment.
1370s	Publications by John Wycliffe, maintaining the bible as the sole criterion of doctrine, and disputing Scriptural foundation for papal authority.
1380-1400	First flourishing of Lollards (followers of Wycliffe).
1381	Rebellion of Wat Tyler.
c.1400	Additional inning of Walland Marsh.
1414	Suppression of Alien Priories; Lollard uprising.
1418	Partial re-conquering of Normandy.
c.1425	Final silting-up of Rhee channel.
1440s-1450s	Loss of French possessions; Wars of the Roses.
1453	End of Hundred Years' War.
1461	Accession of Edward IV.
1462	Granting of charter creating the Liberty of Romney Marsh.
c.1470	Start of inning of Guldeford Marsh.
1483	Aliens restrained from retail trades and handicrafts.
c.1490	Revival of Lollardy.
1505	Dedication of East Guldeford church.
1525	Tyndale translation of New Testament into English.

1534 - 1660 REFORMATION AND PURITANISM

1534	Act of Supremacy, declaring the primacy of Crown rather than papal authority.
1535	Dissolution of religious houses of a value below £200.

1536	Declaration of the Ten Articles, laying down traditional catholic principles of worship. Royal orders also required clergy to observe anti-papal laws, curtailed holy days and ceremonies, discouraged images, relics, miracles and pilgrimages, and required the teaching in English of the articles and the Ten Commandments.
1537	The "Bishop's Book" prepared, setting down an agreed approach to liturgy and practice.
1538	Order to set up the Great Bible (first authorised English version) in every church.
1539	Declaration of the Six Articles, reinforcing traditional catholic liturgical practice.
1540	Dissolution of larger religious houses.
1542	Order for lessons to be read in English.
1543	The "King's Book" prepared, again reinforcing traditional catholic practices with the exception of Papal authority.
1545	Claim by the Crown of chantry incomes for to the duration of Henry VIII's reign.
1547	Accession of Edward VI. Suppression of chantries and guild chapels (2,374 in all), and claim of income by Crown. Many Royal injunctions, including regular sermons against superstition and Papal authority; regular services, paying of tithes, keeping of registers, and study/teaching of Scripture; requirement for a pulpit in each church; Epistle and Gospel to be read in English while kneeling (as opposed to being read in procession); condemning of pictures and all lights except those in front of the Sacrament.
1548	Privy Council proclamations abolishing images and enforcing services in English.
1549	Formal abolition of clerical celibacy. Issuing of first Book of Common Prayer, and enforced use by Act of Uniformity.
1550	Introduction of new Ordinal, and order to destroy altars and replace with wooden tables. Severe injunctions by Bishop Ridley against continuing Romish church practices.
1552	Second Book of Common Prayer and new Act of uniformity, and removal of screens for implementing the new rites.
1553	Declaration of the 42 Articles, with new catechism and primer. Seizure of church plate for king's use; nomination of bishops by letters patent for life or for good behaviour.

	Accession of Mary in July, 1553. Repeal of 1534 Act of Supremacy, and of all laws pertaining to religion passed during the reign of Edward VI. Much imprisonment and removal of bishops for marriage and ill-behaviour.
1554	Repeal of all acts after 1530 against papal authority; full papal pardon given to nation.
1555	Persecutions (burning of 67, including Bishops Ridley and Latimer, two other bishops, and thirteen priests). In this year, the first duties were given to civil parishes (maintenance of highways).
1556-1557	118 burnings, including Archbishop Cranmer. 1557 also saw an important first publication of Puritan principles.
1558	Accession of Elizabeth in November, 1558, followed by release of religious prisoners.
1559-1566	Injunctions and orders, including new Acts of Uniformity and Supremacy, enforcing of compulsory sermons, instruction in catechism, etc. and re-establishment of Edward VI's religious laws. The re-imposing of Edwardian injunctions against images led to much white-washing of church walls.
1561	Order to remove upper parts of screens (eliminating roods), to post the Ten Commandments above the altar table, and to move the table to a suitable position (including into the nave) for communion.
1563	First publication of Thirty-nine Articles.
1568	Revised version of Bible.
1569	Order to remove rood screens and other embellishments entirely.
1570	Queen's excommunication by pope.
1571	Final form of Thirty-nine Articles.
1572	Establishment of the first protestant Presbytery.
1601	First poor laws, making civil parish responsible for relief.
1603	Order to have preaching pulpits in all churches.
1604	Issuing of comprehensive canon laws (141 canons). These again included an order for the Decalogue to be posted; it should be noted, however, that although creed and prayer boards were also often put up, they were never subject of such an order.
c.1620	Widespread introduction of altar rails to protect the table from irreverent treatment.

1633-1641	Laud episcopacy. Laud's concerns included the re-emphasis of the communion table rather than the pulpit as the centre of the church; a focus on the Eucharist (by this time, celebration in many churches was down to once a quarter); an east-end, chancel positioning of the altar; suppression of Protestant Lecturers; and the proclamation of Divine Right.
1640-1660	Puritan revolution and Commonwealth. Widespread removal of images, altar rails, etc. (In 1643, for example, a parliamentary ordinance abolished east-end altars and altar rails, and ordered the relocation of the communion table to a convenient position in the chancel or nave).
1660-1688	Restoration. Re-establishment of the Act of Uniformity and new prayer book (1662), and order to exhibit royal arms in all churches. Many royal Declarations of Indulgences, suspending penalties against Dissenters and their practices. The Declaration of 1672 is used to mark the formal sanction of nonconformity.
1673	Test Act, requiring holders of all Crown offices to be of the Church of England.
1600s-1700s	Widespread private ownership of pews; introduction of box and family pews; use of triple pulpits and galleries, etc.
1829	Repeal of Test Act (emancipating Catholics).
1833-45	Tractarianism (Oxford and Camden Society movements), which aimed at restoring the ideals of the High Church. It is significant that the resulting Victorian renovations of churches (removing box pews and triple pulpits, asserting the importance of the chancel) reflected a particular 19th-century view of the church: it was not, as claimed, a return to mediaeval practice.
1834-1920	Removal of most civil parish responsibilities.
1898-1986	Changes to, and virtual elimination of private rights of patronage to parish churches.

GLOSSARY

Advowson. A perpetual and transferable right to nominate a priest to a specific ecclesiastical living or benefice. Appendant advowsons passed with ownership of a manor or other estate; advowsons in gross could be transferred separately from one owner to another.

Appropriated benefice. Where the parochial income from tithes is taken by an ecclesiastical owner, which in turn pays for a vicar or curate.

Apse. A semicircular termination to a building, usually to a chancel or chapel.

Arcade. A range of arches carried on piers or columns. When attached to a wall, referred to as a blind arcade.

Battlement. A low wall with alternating indentations and raised portions. Also called a crenellation.

Benefice. The independent income which comes with a permanent church office (rectory, vicarage, deanery, prebend, or archeaconry).

Boss. An ornamental knob, often carved, which covers the intersection of ribs in a vault or ceiling.

Box pew. A pew enclosed with high wooden walls and a door, often with seats facing inwards rather than towards the altar or priest. Almost always dating to the 1700s, such pews were usually privately-owned.

Brass, monumental. A gravestone inlaid with brass plates engraved with the effigy of the deceased and a pious inscription. Examples are known to date from 1247 to as late as the 1600s.

Buttress. A mass of masonry or brickwork projecting from or built against a wall to give additional strength.

Canon law. The general law of the church, established by Rome and accepted in part by various synods in England. Canon law remained in force after the Reformation, except as limited by royal prerogative and decrees.

Chancel. The part of the east end of a church in which the main altar is placed. The chancel arch separates the chancel from the nave.

Chantry. An endowment which pays for the singing of masses for the soul of the founder or whoever the founder nominates. A chantry chapel is one kept by the church for the saying of these services.

Choir. The part of the church where divine service is sung, usually forming part of the chancel.

Churchwarden. Originally, the office of the person who took care of the church and the goods needed for the observance of services, and ensured that services were properly and legally carried out.

Clerestory. The upper part of a church's walls, pierced by windows which often overlook the roof of the aisles.

Column. An upright support, circular in plan, and usually slightly tapered.

Constable, parish. The officer in a civil parish who ensures compliance with the law. In local communities often an unpleasant role, and thus held in rotation by the local population.

Crocket. In gothic architecture, a decoration carved in various shapes which projects from the angles of spires, pinnacles, gables, etc.

Crossing. The space at the intersection of the nave, chancel and transepts of a church.

Curate. Technically, anyone appointed by the bishop who has the cure, or care, of souls. In the English church, applied to clergy acting as deputies or assistants to rectors or vicars. Perpetual curates are those appointed where the benefice is owned by a layman (see "Impropriated benefice"), and who cannot be removed by the layman.

Customary tenant. In a manor, a tenant who leased some or all of the lord's freehold lands for a fixed number of years (i.e., having merely the custom or use of the land, and not the freehold).

Demesne land. In a manor, the lands owned freehold by the lord himself. These included his own land, land leased to customary tenants, and the communal waste lands (which were subject to rights of common use by all tenants).

Diocese. The district under the jurisdiction of a bishop.

East end. By convention, that end of the church in which the altar is found. Originally accurate because of the east/west orientation of early churches, but applied to the "altar end" regardless of the actual orientation of the church.

Fiefdom. A mediaeval estate such as a manor, held by virtue of manorial "service".

Freehold tenant. In a manor, a tenant who held his lands by virtue of services or other payments provided to the lord. Provided the service or payment was made, the lord could not deprive such a tenant of his lands.

Gargoyle. A water spout projecting from the roof or a parapet, and carved into a grotesque human or animal figure.

Gemot. An open Anglo-Saxon meeting, often annual, held by the community to decide common matters.

Glebe. The freehold land which formed part of the benefice in a parish.

Impropriated benefice. At the Dissolution, the monasteries' income from "appropriated" parochial tithes passed along with the estates to the Crown, and were either kept by the king or granted to his courtiers. The retention of this income by the new lay owners - previously illegal - is known as "impropriation" to distinguish it from ecclesiastical ownership (or "appropriation").

Incumbent. The holder of a benefice. "Gentry incumbents" were those members of landed families who entered the ministry largely in order to enjoy the family's patronage of various benefices.

Lancet window. A slender pointed-arch window, popular in churches in the early 1200s.

Lectern. The reading-desk or stand from which the Lessons are read in Morning and Evening Prayer. Often in the form of an eagle.

Lintel. A horizontal beam over a door or window, which takes the weight of the wall above.

Manor. In modern times, often used to refer to the area "owned" by a lord. Legally, however, a manor is the set of rights vested in the lord, applying to certain lands and to his jurisdiction over his tenants.

Manorial court. The feudal court, consisting of the lord and his freehold tenants, which regulated the running of the manor.

Minster. An anglicised word for monastery, or a religious establishment with residential priests. The modern use of the word for certain large churches has, of course, lost this original meaning.

Mullion. The upright piece of a window which divides the opening into two or more "lights".

Nave. The part of a church to the west of a chancel, in which the congregation assembles for public worship.

Norman. Period of architecture from the Norman Conquest of 1066 through to the late 1100s.

Oratory. A private chapel, usually in a house, which was used for prayer but which was not consecrated for the celebration of Holy Communion.

Oriel window. A bay window which projects from an upper floor but does not reach to the ground.

Parapet. A low wall which protects against a sudden drop (at the edge of a roof or along a precipitous walkway, etc.).

Parish, detached portion. An area which comes under the jurisdiction of a given parish, but which shares no boundaries with the main portion of that parish. Usually the result of an historical grant of lands to the parish, or the later creation of an intervening parish.

Patron. The person who holds the right of presentation to a benefice.

Pier. A solid masonry support, free-standing to attached to a wall, which is not round in section. Often applied to Romanesque and Gothic pillars which have various sectional profiles.

Pilaster. A shallow pier, attached to and projecting only slightly from a wall.

Piscina. A stone basin with a drain, used for washing the Communion vessels. Usually set into a niche near the altar.

Plinth. The projecting base of a wall or column, either internal or external.

Presentation. The nomination of a priest or minister to a benefice.
Quoins. Stonework at the corner of a building which is laid so that the long and short faces of the stones alternate.

Random rubble. Unhewn building stones or flints, not laid in regular courses.

Rector. The usual title of the incumbent of a parochial benefice, who held all of the original rights and endowments -- the care of the parish, and the whole of the income from the tithes.

Reredos. A wall or screen, usually decorated and of wood or stone, rising behind an altar.

Rib. A projecting band on a ceiling or vault, either structural or purely decorative.

Rood/Rood screen/Rood loft. The Saxon word for a cross or crucifix, referring in churches to a crucifix set up at the east end of the nave and flanked by figures of the Virgin and St. John. In the 1400s, it became usual to place the figures on top of the screen which divided the nave and chancel (hence "rood screen"), along the top of which a narrow gallery was formed (the "rood loft").

Sanctuary. The area immediately surrounding the altar.

Saxon. The period dating from the arrival of the Anglo-Saxons in the 400s to the Norman Conquest of 1066.

Sedilia. Seats for the clergy (generally three, for priest, deacon and subdeacon), built in masonry in the south wall of the chancel.

Seigneur. An alternative name for a feudal lord.

Service, manorial. Payment for the tenancy of manorial lands, either in the form of personal service (often as a knight) or as a monetary payment.

Spandrel. The triangular space formed by the intersection of two arches with the vault of a ceiling.

Stoup. A vessel to contain holy water, placed near the entrance of a church and usually in the form of a shallow dish.

String-course. A continuous projecting horizontal band set in the surface of a wall.

Surveyor, parish. A parochial office, created in the mid 1550s when civil parishes were given the responsibility of maintaining highways.

Tenemental Land. In a manor, lands held by freehold tenants rather than by the lord himself or his "customary tenants".

Tester/Sounding Board. An acoustic canopy above the pulpit.

Thane. A Saxon aristocratic rank; in practice, the lord of the manor.

Tie Beam. A horizontal beam between two walls which connects the feet of the the roof rafters, thus counteracting the outward thrust of the roof which would otherwise push the walls apart.

Tithe. A portion of the parish's income, in kind or as a fixed sum of money, required by law to be given to support a rector or other curate.

Tracery. The ornamental network of stone or wood which decorates the upper part of a window, screen or panel, or which is placed against vaults or blank arches.

Transept. The projecting arms of a cross-shaped church, usually between the chancel and nave. (Occasionally found at the west end of the nave; some churches have two transepts.)

Tympanum. The area above the lintel of a doorway and the arch above.

Tythingman. The manorial equivalent of a parish constable, responsible for the administration of the regional area called a "tything".

Undercroft. A vaulted space below an upper room; sometimes underground.

Vault. An arched ceiling of stone and brick, sometimes imitated in wood or plaster.

Vestry, parish. A kind of parochial parliament which is made up of all rate-paying parishioners. The annual vestry meeting appointed parochial officials, exercising control over their activities, and also acted as a parochial synod to deal with local ecclesiastical matters.

Vicar. The title of an incumbent whose parochial income from the tithe has been appropriated or impropriated. In practice, vicars had equal power to full rectors, the only difference being that the title of a vicarage indicated that the parish had been deprived of the major part of its ancient endowment.

Voussoirs. The wedge-shaped stones or bricks used in constructing an arch.

West end. The opposite end of a church from the altar, by convention applied to this end regardless of the actual orientation of the church.

BIBLIOGRAPHY AND FURTHER READING

1. CIVIL AND ECCLESIASTICAL PARISHES

Less has been written on the development of parishes - both civil and ecclesiastical - than might be expected. Most detailed information is found in a multitude of different works, although a good starting point is always the various articles and bibliographies given in the Oxford Dictionary of the Christian Church.

An excellent general picture of the development of parishes can be found in the recently-published "Discovering Parish Boundaries" by Winchester. More detail can, however, be obtained by returning to the work of Canon Addleshaw, upon which a great deal of further work has been based. With regard to civil parishes, the work of Bryan Keith-Lucas on the local government before the reforms of the 1890s is obviously of great interest.

Addleshaw, G.W.O.
Rectors, Vicars and patrons in 12th and 13th Century Canon Law. (St. Anthony's Hall Publications, IX, 1956.)
The Beginnings of the Parochial System. (St. Anthony's Hall Publications, III, 1953.)
The Development of the Parochial System from Charlemagne (768-814) to Urban II (1088-1099). (St. Anthony's Hall Publications, VI, 1954.)
The Early Parochial System and the Divine Office. (Mowbray, 1957)

Cross, F.L. and Livingstone, E.A., eds.
The Oxford Dictionary of the Christian Church. (Oxford, 1983.)

Cutts, E.L.
A Dictionary of the Church of England. (London, c.1890.)
Parish Priests and their people in the Middle Ages in England. (London, 1914.)

Dale, Sir William.
The Law of the Parish Church. (London, 5th ed., 1975.)

Gasquet, A.
Parish Life in Mediaeval England. (The Antiquary's Books, 1906.)

Goodenough, Simon.
The Country Parson. (Newton Abbott, 1983.)

Johnson, Theodore.
The Parish Guide. (London, 1887.)

Keith-Lucas, Bryan.
English Local Government in the 19th and 20th Centuries. (London, 1977.)
Parish Affairs: The Government of Kent under George III. (London, 1986.)
The Unreformed Local Government System. (London, 1980.)

Macleod, Donald.
The Parochial System. (St. Giles's Lecture Series VI, 1886.)

Macmorran, Kenneth M. and Elphinstone, Kenneth J.T.
A Handbook for Church wardens and Parochial Church Councillors. (London, 1983.)

Phythian-Adams, Charles.
Continuity, Fields and Fission. (University of Leicester, 1978.)

Seebohn, F.
The English Village Community. (1883.)

Smith, Frank.
A Genealogical Gazeteer of England. (Baltimore, 1982.) Includes a useful list of parishes, with their status under archdeaconries, as peculiars, etc.

Thompson, P.D.
Parish and Parish Church: Their Place and Influence in History. (Baird Lecture/1935, pub. 1948.)

Winchester, Angus.
Discovering Parish Boundaries. (Princes Risborough, Bucks: Shire Publications, 1990.)

2. CHURCHES, ARCHITECTURE AND FITTINGS

The physical impact of liturgy upon the design and embellishment of churches, while always acknowledged, falls somewhere between the fields of architectural and liturgical history. This is unfortunate, as it has arguably been the single most important influence on the layout and embellishment of church buildings. To explore the field one must refer to works from both disciplines, but many general queries can probably be resolved by simple reference to the Oxford Dictionary of the Christian Church or other general works.

Addleshaw, G.W.O. and Etchels, Frederick.
The Architectural Setting of Anglican Worship. (Faber, 1948.)

Brooks, N.
The Early History of the Church of Canterbury: Christ Church from 597 to 1066. (Leicester, 1984.)

Cuming, G.J.
A History of Anglican Liturgy. (London, 1969.)

Summerson, John.
Architecture in Britain: 1530-1830. (Harmondsworth, 5th ed., 1969.)

Yarwood, Doreen.
A Chronology of Western Architecture. (London, 1987.)

3. TOPOGRAPHICAL WORKS

Specific topographical information on individual parish churches can usually be found in the small pamphlets purchased from each parish church, or in more general pamphlets published about Romney Marsh. These have not been listed below.

Brentnall, Margaret.
The Cinque Ports and Romney Marsh. (London, 2nd edition, 1980.)

Cunliffe, Prof. B.W.
"The Evolution of Romney Marsh: a Preliminary Statement", in Thompson, Archaeology and Coastal Change, pp 37-55. London: Society of Antiquaries, 1980.

Derville, M. Teichman.
The Level and Liberty of Romney Marsh. (Ashford, 1936.) Includes a good list of manors and names associated with them, and reproduces charters of Edward IV.

Eddison, Jill and Green, Christopher, eds.
Romney Marsh: Evolution, Occupation, Reclamation. Oxford: Oxford University Committee for Archaeology, Monograph No 24, 1988.

Finn, Arthur, ed.
Records of Lydd. (Ashford, 1911.)

Forbes, Duncan.
The Fifth Continent. (Hythe, 1984.)

Furley, Robert.
"An Outline of the History of Romney Marsh", in Archaeologia Cantiana, Vol. XIII. (London, 1880.)

Hasted.
History of Kent. (1790.) The major county history, upon which almost all other historical work has been based.

Holloway, William.
The History of Romney Marsh. (London, 1849.) A rare book. Very useful, but difficult to use as it is not indexed.

Homan, Roger.
The Victorian Churches of Kent. (Chichester, 1984.)

Newman, John.
The Buildings of England: Northeast and East Kent. (Harmondsworth, 2nd ed., 1976.)

Robinson, Canon Scott.
"Churches in Romney Marsh". (Archaeologica Cantiana, Vol. XIII, 1880.)
Victoria County History of the County of Kent. (London, 1926.) Volume II deals with
Ecclesiastical History. Parochial histories of the V.C.H. for Kent have unfortunately never been produced.

Tatton-Brown, Tim.
"Church Building on Romney Marsh in the Later Middle Ages", in Archaeologia Cantiana, Volume CVII (1989), pp. 253-265. Gloucester: Alan Sutton Publishing, for Kent Archaeological Society, 1989.

4. MANORS AND MANORIAL LAW

Goodeve, L.A.
The Modern Law of Real Property. (London, 1906.)

Hardy Ivamy, E.R., ed.
Mozley and Whiteley's Law Dictionary. (London, 10th ed, 1988.)

Hart, Sir William O. and Garner, Prof.
J.F. Hart's Introduction to the Law of Government and Administration. (London, 1973.)

Vinogradoff, P.
Villeinage in England. (1892.)
The Growth of the Manor. (1902.)

INDEX

Advowsons 15
Aldred, Rev. C. R. 40
All Souls, Oxford 60
Arminand, William 44
Arms, Anne 61, 68
    George II 42
    George III 35, 45, 46, 54, 62, 69
    George IV 49
Arrouaise Abbey 62
Augustine, Saint 11

Balston, Richard James 28, 35
Barham, Rev. Richard 73
Barnham, Francis 28
    Martin 28, 35
Becket, Saint Thomas 34, 50
Bedingfield, Capt Timothy 46
Benefices, appropriated 15
Benson, E. F. 28, 68
Benson, Archbishop 28
Bilsington 16, 28, 31, 34-35, 37, 64
Bilsington Priory 34, 35, 78
Blackmanstone 24
Bonnington 16, 24, 31, 36-37, 64
Brenzett 16, 38-40, 75
Brockman, Rev. R. D. 16, 40
    Rev. T. 40
Brookland 13, 22, 41-43, 51
Bucler, Walter 39
Burmarsh 13, 16, 24, 31, 44-45, 77

Cameron, F. Martin 35
Canterbury, Abbey 41, 44, 46, 64, 74, 75
    Cathedral 41, 65
    Priory 50, 64
Chantry chapels 27, 28, 67, 78
Church, Introduction to England 11-12
    Development of parishes 12-14
Churchwardens 9, 18
Cinque Ports 21, 55, 78
Clarke, Joseph 35
Cnut 66, 77
Constable, parish 8-9, 18
Cooke, Richard 48
Cooper, Rev. R. G. 35

Deffray, Rev. John 62
Dekyn, Thomas 40
Dering family 24
Dymchurch 16, 31, 46-47

Eanswith, Saint 39
Eastbridge 24
East Guldeford 16, 22, 23, 29, 48-49, 78, 79
Eastwell 24
Eden, F. Conrad 47
Edgar 12, 77
Edmund 12, 77
Edmunds, Hannah 35
Edward the Confessor 13, 77
Edward I 15, 18, 78
Edward IV 22, 79
Egbert, Archbishop of York 11
Ethelred 13, 77

Fagge family 40
Fairfield 14, 16, 22, 31, 50-51, 78
Farmer, Henry 48
Fecamp Abbey 66
Finch family 24
Fisher, Thomas 40
Fowle, John 46
Furnese, Sir Henry 50

Gibson, Joseph 35
Godfrey, Thomas 56
Guldeford, Sir Richard 48
Guynes Abbey 39

Hales, Sir James 37
Hamon, Thomas 68
Haut, Jane 24
Henry III 66
Henry VII 58
Henry VI 22
Henry VIII 16
Holynoke, William 60
Honychild 24
Hope 16
Horne Chapel 28
Hurst 16

Ibbotson, Rev. Edmund 45
Ips, John 62
    Margaret 62
Ivychurch 14, 28, 31, 52-54, 78

Jamys, Matilda 69
    William George 69
Jordan, John 34

Kempe, Archbishop of York 39
Kenardington 24

Lamb family 49, 67, 68
Lambard, Thomas 61
Lanfranc 78
Laud, Archbishop 41, 42
Liturgy and church form 27, 30-31, 40, 42, 69, 72, 75, 80-82
Lixmoore, Justice 28
Lydd 22, 28, 31, 55-57

Magna Carta 18, 78
Manorial law 8, 17-18
Meryle, Sir Walter de 55
de Moraunt family 24
Moyle family 24

Nesbit, Edith M. 70
Newchurch 31, 58-59

Odo of Bayeux 64
Offa 55, 64
Orgarswick 44
Oyler, T. H. 62

Packmanstone 24
Papillon family 16, 37
Parishes, civil 7, 17-19, 81-82
    ecclesiastical 11-16
Patronage 15-16, 82
Peckham family
Playden 48, 49
Plomer, john 41
Potigney Priory 60
Presentation, rights of 15
Property law 24

Rhee channel 21, 39, 41, 72, 74, 78, 79
Rider family 35
Rolff, Richard 54
Romenal, de family 62
Romney, New 23, 31, 55, 60-61
Romney, Old 16, 31, 62-63, 72
Romney Marsh, charter 22, 79
    Lords of 21, 24, 46
    nature of/storms 21, 23, 55, 60
    number of churches 14, 69
Ruckinge 13, 64-65, 77
Rumwold, Saint 36
Rye 16, 22, 23, 28, 31, 66-68

Sackville family 67
Saint John, Knights Hospitallers 36
Saint Mary in the Marsh 31, 69-71
Smuggling 54, 65, 72
Smyth, Thomas 61
Snargate 13, 72-73, 75
Somery, Roger de 34
Somner, William 40
Stanley, Thomas 55
St Leger, Anthony 28
Stuppenye, Clement 56
    Richard 61
Surveyor, Parish 19

Theodore, Archbishop 11, 17, 77
Thomas, John 55
Tiltman, Mary 68
Tintern Abbey 55
Tinton 24
Tookey, Thomas 61
Turner family 16, 37
Twysden, Roger 24

Vestry, parish 8, 9, 17, 19
Victorian restorations 30, 35, 37, 40, 45, 46, 56, 61, 62-63

Walland Marsh 21, 23, 39, 50, 79
War damage 43, 47, 56, 66, 68
Warehorne 24, 73
Wentworth, Rev. John 40
William I 13, 64, 77
William II 13
Winchelsea 23, 66, 68
Wyatt, Sir Thomas 24
Wye, College of 39